'Lots of people talk about "following Jesu
what it looks like in practice, this book
Bible and applied to everyday life. It is
inspiration while being considered, rich
to find a book that is accessible and yet able to take us deeper in our relationship with God – you've found one here.'
Andy Croft, Joint Senior Pastor, Soul Survivor Watford

'God makes sense of who you are at the deepest level, so the dreams and purpose God has for you have the power to bring about a stunning revolution at the core of your life. In this brilliant book, Martin powerfully and practically helps you to explore how finding yourself in God's orbit will open you up to the life you were always made to live.'
Rachel Gardner, Director of National Work, Youthscape

'Martin Saunders is a brilliant guide for anyone trying to get their heads around following Jesus in a way that really works. I trust him, respect him and like him a lot. I think that, after reading this book, you'll feel the same way too.'
Pete Greig, 24-7 Prayer International and Emmaus Rd Church

'Ever since I heard Martin extol the concept behind satellites, I was hooked. This is exactly the whole-life Christianity we all need. Goodbye to the quick-fix, just-add-boiling-water experience – what we desire more than anything for ourselves and particularly for our young people is a compelling, creative, beautiful and challenging vision of life lived in every way and direction around and for Jesus.'
The Revd Canon Chris Russell, the Archbishop of Canterbury's Advisor for Evangelism and Witness

'This is my new go-to book to recommend for young people. If you're wrestling with your faith, or curious as to whether there is a God worth revolving your whole life around, *We Are Satellites* is worth a read. The way this book is written so naturally and passionately, you can tell that Martin has decades of wisdom, experience and conversations with young people about faith behind his words. This book will kick-start your journey towards trusting God or energize you to keep going, to keep discovering more of Jesus and his vision for the world. I hope that every young person reads this book and then shares it with a friend. The more of us who can know and live as if we are satellites orbiting around God and his love, the better the world will be.'

Miriam Swanson, Global Student Mission Leader, Fusion

Martin Saunders is Director of Innovation at Youthscape, Youth Team Leader at St Mary's Church, Reigate, and the author of many books, including *The Man You're Made to Be* (SPCK). He has been involved in youth ministry for nearly two decades, including more than ten years as editor of *Youthwork* magazine. Martin is married to Jo and they have four children.

WE ARE SATELLITES

How to put God at the centre of your life

Martin Saunders

First published in Great Britain in 2020

Society for Promoting Christian Knowledge
36 Causton Street
London SW1P 4ST
www.spck.org.uk

British Library Cataloguing-in-Publication Data
A catalogue record for this book is available from the British Library

ISBN 978-0-281-08423-4
eBook ISBN 978-0-281-08424-1

Typeset by Manila Typesetting Company
First printed in Great Britain by Jellyfish Print Solutions
Subsequently digitally printed in Great Britain

eBook by Manila Typesetting Company

Produced on paper from sustainable forests

For the amazing young people of St Mary's, Reigate

Contents

Acknowledgements

I couldn't have written this book, or at least the version you're holding, without a massive amount of help. So thanks to Jen Coleman, Stephen Fenwick, Ali Martin, Charles Merritt, Steven Mitchell and Robbie Thomson for reading it at various stages, being honest, and helping me to avoid certain disaster. Thanks to Tony Collins and Elizabeth Neep at SPCK for saintly levels of patience and encouragement through the commissioning, writing and editing processes. Thanks to the teams at Youthscape and St Mary's Reigate for constantly inspiring me along the way, and, perhaps most of all, thanks to Jo and our kids for frequently sacrificing fun times together so that I could get a bit more of the book written.

Finally: writing a book is always a risk, and I would never feel brave enough to take it if I didn't have a pretty amazing group of encouraging friends behind me. So to all of them – and particularly Steve Cole, Ruth Mawhinney and Adam Prior – thanks for having my back, and for encouraging me at moments when I felt as if I had nothing left in the tank.

Introduction

You are one in 7.7 billion. You're nobody, a random collection of atoms, evolved into human shape by some cosmic fluke, sitting on a spinning rock that by astronomical chance happened to be able to support life. There's no real plan, point or order to your life, and you could die at any moment. From nothing you came, to nothing you'll return, and it won't matter, because you don't matter – nothing does. It all just happens. *Or* . . .

Or there is more to life than that. Maybe it doesn't just happen; maybe there's something bigger and greater behind it all. Perhaps your life, and what you do with it, actually matters. And it could possibly be true that you are not here by chance at all, but by design; created, not fluked into existence. Standing on a handcrafted planet that's the centre-point of an ordered universe, brought into being not by luck but by a Magnificent Being, greater and more powerful than any of us could ever possibly imagine. And if that *is* true, then it could also be true that this great Creator – this *God* – placed you into the heart of that creation. Not random, not ordinary, but utterly unique and extraordinarily special.

You *are* one in 7.7 billion. But the God who made every single one calls you by name. He calls you into orbit around himself. For you, my friend, are made to be a *satellite*.

1.
ALL OR NOTHING

There are some things that shouldn't have an in-between option.

Like music; you shouldn't do music half-heartedly. You can't just pick up a guitar, strum along with a couple of YouTube tutorials and then declare yourself ready to join a band. You're not going to be a very good rock star if you've only learnt three chords.

Or think about sport: your teammates won't think much of you if you wander aimlessly around whatever pitch or court you're playing on, vaguely interested in receiving the ball, but obsessing over whether your hair looks right today. Sport demands focus, energy and attention – nobody ever won anything through skill alone.

These things only really work if you choose to give them 100 per cent. Invest any less, and your band will throw you out after one rehearsal, and at some point they'll stop picking you for that team no matter how good your hair is. All or nothing – that's your choice.

The same goes for faith in God. It only really works if you're *all in*. Serving and submitting to God doesn't work as a bolt-on; as one interest among many to sit alongside your secret passion for Korean pop music and the fact that you quite like pandas. Christianity tells us that God is involved in revolution, turning the world upside down, and using regular humans like you and me as his means for doing so. And revolutions aren't staffed by part-timers. If we really want to be part of God's great plan to remake the world, it's going to demand everything we've got.

So that's the key question, and really it's the main challenge of this book (just in case you're the sort of person who only reads the first couple of pages). Are you going to give God everything, or are you going to give him nothing? Because that halfway house option isn't really worth your time.

Before we get to that question, however, we need to address the bigger and more fundamental one that sits behind it. It's the question that every single person in history has probably asked at least once, and its answer is perhaps the most important piece of information that anyone could ever possibly know.

Is there a God?

A pretty deep question, that. Because if you were truly to arrive at an answer, surely it would define the course of your life. If there *isn't* a God, then religious faith is a complete waste of time. No one should ever go anywhere near a church, bother crossing themselves before stepping on to a sports pitch or go to a Christian funeral ever again. If there isn't a God we should throw all those necklaces away, take the saints' names off our schools and never, ever pray again – even if our plane is going down. If there isn't a God then Christian faith is ridiculous; a complete waste of any sensible human being's time.

There's another option though. If there *is* a God then that changes everything too. That's the most important thing you could ever realize or know. If there *is* a God – a God who made you, loves you and somehow wants to know you personally – then your life would have to look dramatically different as a result of knowing that he's real. Right? You would let that piece of information become the central driving force behind everything you do.

Let's take a very different example. If you knew that someone wanted to kill you, then it's fair to say that this piece of knowledge would have a serious impact on the way you lived your daily life. You'd be talking to the police regularly, and you might be asking them for round-the-clock protection. You'd spend everything you had on home security; you might even hire a bodyguard. You'd enrol in ju-jitsu classes; you'd sleep inside an impenetrable vault (if you happened to have access to one). You would live every moment of every day in a constant, heightened state of fear and awareness; it would define your entire lifestyle.

No one is trying to kill you. But if you happen to buy into the Christian story, then someone *is* relentlessly pursuing you. It's just that rather than trying to kill you, he's aiming to bring you to life, and to recruit you to a world-transforming movement where you can help bring others to life too.

If you truly believe that God is real, then you can't just be vaguely comforted by the nice thought and leave it there. If God is real then he made you, and if he made you then he has intentions for you. If God is real then you're not here by accident, and instead there's a reason and a purpose for your life. And so it's only natural that the way in which you live your life would be radically influenced by that piece of information. Instead of running from danger, you'd be running towards hope; instead of taking steps to combat and defend yourself against hatred, you would be embracing and sharing an offer of unconditional love.

But the question remains: *is* God real?

I've believed that he is since I was 14 years old. I was a podgy, unspectacular teenager, attending an all-boys' school in south west London. My experience of school was largely unpleasant: bullying, slightly sadistic teachers, and a seriously strict rulebook. One of those rules was that you couldn't spend any of the break times inside the safety of the school buildings – which, when you're a target for both bullies and unhinged physics teachers, is bad news.

One particularly wet and miserable day, however, as I stood shivering and sheltering under my school blazer in the corner of the school field, I found a loophole. I discovered that you *were* allowed to enter the school building at lunchtime, provided you were part of a recognized club or society. Being uniformly awful at all sports ruled out most lunchtime activities, and I didn't want to join the chess club or the rare-stamp-collecting society. But one advert caught my attention. It said: 'Jesus: Good, mad, bad or God? Come and decide for yourself at Christian Union – Wednesday 1 pm.'

I'll be completely honest with you. I had zero interest in the answer to that question. If it's possible, less than zero. All I wanted was a place to shelter from the rain, and maybe a flat surface on which to play my table-top cricket scoring game.* I didn't care at all about Jesus; I didn't believe in God, but not only was the Christian Union an indoor club (with radiators), but it was actually held in my own form room. This would be my ticket out of the rain.

**Yes, I was a nerd.*

When I arrived that first week, I was pounced upon by a pack of over-enthusiastic welcomers. They rarely saw new blood, and my appearance was apparently the answer to their prayers. Boys four years older than me were smiling politely and calling me by my *actual* name; it was *weird*. So, a little freaked out but pleased to have made it through their non-existent vetting system, I made my way to the back row of the class. I had no intention of listening to the talk, so got out my pencil and paper to play out the fourth one-day international between England and Pakistan.*

See above.

I don't know at what point I stopped focusing on the cricket, but after a while I became aware of myself listening to the guest speaker, a local youth worker called Terry. He was a small but charismatic man, and quite striking to look at – like a very, very distant cousin of Tom Cruise (or perhaps like someone had tried to draw Tom Cruise from memory). He was funny and intelligent and, contrary to my preconception of Christians, he was fairly normal. His talk wasn't loud and preachy, it was calm and reasonable. So, despite trying not to, I sat and listened.

Terry was – as promised by that poster – trying to answer the question of who Jesus was. Again, I'll be honest: this was not a question that I had previously been bothered about (you may well feel the same way). To me, Jesus was either a figure from history or a bearded, friendly faced guy from children's picture books. I had never wondered if he was mad, or bad, or anything else. Terry on the other hand seemed very serious about the whole thing. He said that if you applied logic, and looked at the life of Jesus as recorded by history, you could start to see that there was only one explanation for who he was.

Here's how his argument roughly went: most people look at Jesus and think, 'He's just a good man, and he inspires me to do good.' Which is fine, until you start to think about it. Because not only did Jesus instruct people to do weird and apparently unkind things like leave their families behind and follow him, but after a while he started claiming to be the Son of God. And the only situation in which that is really considered acceptable, good behaviour is in the unlikely circumstance that it's true. So that sort of rules out the idea that he was simply a good guy.

From there, you obviously leap to the opposite extreme – that he was evil. But, hang on – this is a guy who travelled around healing people, filling them with hope and saying wise and beautiful things that now form the basis of most of our morals and laws. Not only does the Bible never record him doing *anything* wrong, the history books – and there are a lot of them that cover the period of his life – don't remember him doing anything remotely evil either. No one really buys the concept of 'Evil Jesus', do they?

Terry – who, by the way, borrowed this whole thing from a famous writer whom we'll come on to – said that logically, if he was neither good nor bad, you might imagine that he was in fact mad. Random, chaotic, crazy Jesus. The problem with this one is that he was also one of the wisest people who ever lived – as I say, most of the things he's recorded as saying are now viewed not just as common sense but as signposts to the right kind of life. Treat others like you'd want to be treated, love your neighbour – that sort of thing. Not only that, but Jesus' life on earth had a quite spectacularly clever dimension to it – he fulfilled huge numbers of prophecies about the coming Messiah that were written long before he was born. What this means is that people made predictions about where he'd be, what he'd do and say, and how things would happen, and then he made every single one of them true. A person with profound mental health problems could not possibly do that; arguably even an evil genius would struggle, and we've already ruled that option out.

Logically, Terry said, that left only one option: that when Jesus said he was the Son of God, he was telling the truth. Not crazy, not a liar, but actually the Lord of all things. Rationally speaking, the historical character Jesus must also have been the Jesus written about in the Bible.

At that moment, it was as if a switch flicked in my head and a voice whispered in my ear: this is true. And not only that, but I almost immediately realized that if it *was* true, everything in my life needed to change as a result. Because if this was true, then I had lived 14 years without seeing that there was a whole other dimension to the universe – one more important and powerful than anything I already knew. If this was true, it was the most important thing in the world.

So at the end of the session, and to his total amazement, I walked to the front of the room, took Terry to one side and said, 'I think I believe this.'

It may be that you also read the argument above, and are somewhat persuaded by it. And though to some extent this means that you're now free to skip the rest of this chapter, *don't.* While this is still one of the reasons that – more than 25 years later – I still firmly believe that Christianity is true, it isn't the *only* reason. In fact, when you've only got one big reason for believing in God, I fear you often end up in a bit of trouble.

Have you ever put up a tent? I'm not talking about the pop-up *Finding Nemo* one that you had when you were four. I mean a real tent, designed to protect you from the elements, keep your stuff dry, and remind you never to have another holiday in England. I have put up many tents in the course of my life, and I have also observed many other people trying to do the same thing. It would be fair to say that there is some variance in the level of commitment and effort that different people apply to this task.

For some people, a few pegs and a pole are all that is required. They don't even bother driving those things in with a mallet, the mavericks. Others are more sensible, and at least follow the minimum recommendations, pegging out every corner of the canvas and making sure the fabric is taut. Then there's another kind of tent-erector, and I'm prepared to admit that I'm definitely in this camp.* We take no chances, ensuring that our temporary dwellings are put up so robustly that if a monsoon hit or we were unexpectedly asked to live inside for a year, they would not fall down or blow away. We drive in every peg (and some extra pegs we bought); we pull out all of those yellow rope things and create trip hazards in every direction; we make sure that there's not even a remote possibility of the inner and outer layers touching and compromising the waterproofing. We are awful, boring people, and you should never invite us to parties.

**If there is a worse joke in this book, I will be disappointed with myself.*

There is a point to all this. I think there are lots of good arguments for the existence of God. Many different reasons to have faith, which together make up a more and more compelling overall reason to say, 'Yes, I believe this.' Each reason is like another peg around the tent of our faith. As we build up and understand more of these reasons for why Jesus really is the Son of God, and why this God really did make us and love us, we become more and more confident that we're on the right path. And that path inevitably starts to lead somewhere.

This is all really useful because – to stretch the canvas of the camping metaphor just a couple of inches further – sometimes in life the storms come. Things take an unexpected and uncomfortable turn; we get betrayed, let down, bereaved or broken. Those moments of pain and disappointment often cause us to ask big questions: things like 'Why, God?' (which is a really good question) and even 'Are you really there, God?' Now, when we come to ask that second question, the number of pegs we've got in the ground starts to become important. If you've only really got one good reason for believing in God, then the strong winds of grit and grief can send your tent spiralling into the sky, *Wizard of Oz* style. Much better to have all the guy ropes and extra pegs you can find.*

**Jesus tells a story that I've pretty much ripped off here. It's the one about the wise man who built his house upon the rock. You can find the story in Matthew 7.24–27. I added the tents.*

There are many other very good reasons why I believe we can have faith in the God of the Bible. Each one on its own maybe only pegs out one corner of the tent, but together they start to create a canopy under which we can place our entire lives. What follows is not a complete list of those good reasons, but it's a fair start – to which you are free to add your own. For ease of future reference, I've numbered them 1–9.

1 ***The created world.*** Don't worry, I'm not about to start an argument against evolution or suggest dinosaur bones were put there as part of a conspiracy. All I'm going to say is this: look out of your window. Even if you live in the middle of the most concreted of cities, life is everywhere, in all its incredible and varied forms. The weird bug thing on the outside (hopefully) of your window; the weed poking through the crack in your pavement. And, when you get out to the countryside: rolling hills filled with a thousand different species of plant and creature; glistening streams of water all somehow connected to a sea full of a million secrets. That's not even to mention mountains, rainforests, canyons, icebergs, volcanos – majestic wonders each with their own unique and brilliant ecosystem. This planet is impossibly complex and beautiful, only supporting life because its orbit keeps it the perfect distance from an orb of fire that heats it just enough without burning it to a crisp.

The Bible even goes so far as to say that you've got no excuse (Romans 1.24) if you can't see the hand of a creator behind it all.

To me at least, it seems ridiculous to imagine that a planet this perfect wasn't designed and built. The chances of it happening accidentally seem astronomical.

2 ***Miracles happen.*** I'm not talking about the miraculous triumph of the human spirit over adversity here – I'm referring to actual, scientifically unexplainable, miraculous occurrences. Churches all over the world frequently report these: impossible healings from sickness and injury, mind-blowing coincidences, people surviving utterly hopeless situations. The Christian faith says that God is real and that he is at work in the world today; it stands to reason that his work might sometimes look supernatural, disobeying the laws of the world as we understand it. There are a million stories of this nature, and yet generally people are sceptical about them. That's understandable of course – especially when some people abuse the promise of 'miracle healings' for the purpose of financial exploitation. So let me say this: I've seen several people physically healed; I've known coincidences happen which seem too perfect to be random. Make your own mind up, but my considered view after 25 years of following Jesus is that miracles happen, today.

3 ***The Bible adds up.*** Of all the reasons to believe on this list, I understand that 'because the Bible says so' seems to offer the weakest argument. If you don't believe the Bible is truly the inspired word of God, then how can it be used to prove his existence? What's incredible about the Bible, however, is how it all hangs together. Sixty-six books, telling one incredible, complex story across thousands of years: a story that somehow makes sense to us today, and has to every generation since it was written. On a grand scale it spends 39 books setting up the main event – the coming of Jesus – and then another 27 explaining who he was and what that means for us. When seen through

that lens, despite being written by scores of different people, it manages to form a single shape with a simple coherent message: that God is love. And when you break that great narrative down into tiny chunks, you find wisdom that actually helps us to live our everyday lives. A passage, or even a single verse of the Bible, will always have something real and relevant to say; what other millennia-old text can claim that? The Bible works like no other book because it was drawn together by God and is somehow still infected with his power – making it the only book in existence that is somehow alive.

4 ***Lots of smart people believe this.*** I am not – as you will doubtless already have figured out – the world's most intelligent man. I was thoroughly average throughout my school life, and for many years I believed that when people said cappuccino they were talking about a 'cup of chino' (I don't know what chino is). So, to some extent, you'd be pretty foolish to trust what I think about the world. That's why I like to do what Sir Isaac Newton called 'standing on the shoulders of giants'. There are some incredibly intelligent people – both living and dead – who dedicated themselves to this great question of the existence of God, and ended up concluding that the Bible is true, that Jesus is who he says he is, and that our role in the universe is as children of God. These people include C. S. Lewis, the author of the Narnia books, and also the man who came up with the good/mad/bad/ God argument that changed my mind. His friend J. R. R. Tolkien, who wrote the *Lord of the Rings* trilogy, was also a Christian; two greats of literature and intellectual firepower who spent their evenings together chewing over the complexities of Christian theology. Giants from every field of the arts came to the same conclusions, from the composer J. S. Bach to the painters Michelangelo and Van Gogh. Great political brains like Winston Churchill and Barack Obama did likewise. What's perhaps surprising is

the number of great scientists who believed in the Bible too: Faraday, Newton, Pascal, Pasteur – and more recently Francis Collins, who discovered the genes linked to a range of human diseases. These names will continue to fill the pages of science textbooks for centuries to come – yet they all believed in a God behind the science. And look, since it's nice to have other kinds of heroes, it's also worth mentioning the many Christians in sport and entertainment. Movie stars Chris Pratt, Letitia Wright and Mark Wahlberg; musicians Marcus Mumford, Kanye West and Stormzy; sports icons Jürgen Klopp, Steph Curry, Gabby Douglas and Alisson Becker. All of these people share the firm conviction that the God of the Bible is real – and knowing that they've also done the hard work of thinking through and arriving at this conclusion can help us to do the same.

5 ***The wisdom, character and life of Jesus.*** He is absolutely the greatest man who ever lived. Not only did Jesus spend years travelling around on foot, performing miracles, healing people and filling them with hope, but the things that he said were so profound that they're not only talked about today but are still used as the best guidance for living a good and happy life. Look out for your neighbour; treat others as you'd wish to be treated; put others first and you'll find that it really is better to give than to receive . . . his sayings and teachings have survived 2,000 years of interrogation and still prove to be genius-level. He's the guru that every other guru looks up to; he's Yoda, Einstein, Confucius and Socrates all rolled into one. Now, the thing is, history tells us that this man existed *for sure* – there's way more evidence that he existed than there is for anyone else who lived in a similar time period. The question is: who was he? And to return to the argument that convinced me to follow him, there's just no way that a mere mortal was *that good*. It's actually logical that he was the Son of God.

6 ***Changed lives.*** The journey of Christian faith isn't about an overnight switch; one day you're living selfishly, not caring who you hurt, and the next you're floating around like a saint. Instead, it's a process of slow transformation from being the sort of person who lives only in the here and now, to being someone who has a greater perspective and a deep sense of meaning and contentment. That can look a million different ways, and I've seen so many versions: my friend who was a cocaine-addicted East End thug, who met Jesus in a car park after contemplating suicide, and now travels the world telling people about him; a woman I know who spent years as an always angry atheist, who admits she eventually 'gave in' to what she knew deep down all along, and is now the most chilled-out person you could meet. These stories and so many others are different, and yet there's one familiar thread: when people say 'yes' to Christianity, they slowly begin to change for the better. They become kinder, more loving, less selfish, and with a deeper sense of happiness. This doesn't happen in a moment, but over years and years – and it's this steady, slow but repeated transformation that increases my belief that all of this is true and that God is behind the change.

7 ***The good that the Church does, and has done.*** That's right, I'm a fan of the Church. Now, of course if we look back through history, or even around the world, we see that the Church isn't always on the side of good – or even God. Sometimes the organized aspect of religion has been manipulated for terrible reasons – it's been used to subdue and control people, and even as a justification for war. But don't let those awful examples – important as they are – fool you; for the most part, the Church has been responsible for some wonderful things, for thousands of years. Ensuring the poor are fed, the sick are cared for, and even that the most socially excluded people get the chance of human connection. Motivated by their faith, and strengthened by the supernatural

power of God, churches and individual Christians have been responsible for everything from the establishment of justice to the creation of hospitals and schools, through to the ending of slavery. On its own the Church doesn't prove the existence of God, but it does demonstrate that when the immense wisdom of his Bible is put into practice, and people come together in his name, incredible things tend to happen.

8 ***Answered prayer.*** There are many, many stories that appear to demonstrate that prayer is powerful. Some of them are massive. The 'miracle' of Dunkirk for instance – the Second World War turning point where British forces somehow made it back from heavy defeat in France – coincided with a National Day of Prayer across Great Britain. Some of them are comparatively tiny, and perhaps it's these, strangely, that are most likely to build our faith; tiny stories like this one . . .

When my eldest son was six years old, he went with me to the local supermarket. When we were there he was frightened by a larger-than-life woman who shouted in his face about how cute he was (she was a little eccentric); I'd never met or seen her before. He tried to suppress his feelings, but he ended up bursting into tears as soon as she left the shop. When we got home a couple of hours later, it was time to put him to bed, and before I turned the light out, he asked if I could pray with him. His prayer request was simple: that 'the loud lady would know that she upsets children when she shouts like that, and that she'd stop doing it'. I didn't want to disappoint him, so I said the prayer – with zero confidence that it was even possible for God to answer it. A second after I uttered the 'amen' there was – honestly, and I'm not exaggerating in any way – a knock at our front door. My son asked if this would be the woman, coming to apologize; I gently told him that no, that wasn't possible, and kissed him goodnight.

I opened the door expecting to see a friend or neighbour. In fact, it *was* the loud woman from the supermarket. It turned out that she was a local councillor, lobbying people to re-elect her, and tonight she'd decided to go door-to-door. There are tens of thousands of homes in my town but, as insane chance would have it, she ended up on my front step. So when she asked if she could count on my vote, I changed the subject and told her about how upset my son had been because of her brashness. She was very apologetic and promised to consider her behaviour in future. Moments later, a little voice came from upstairs: 'Was that the loud lady from the supermarket?' Almost in total disbelief, I had to tell him, 'Yes.'

From that day on, there's been no doubt in my son's mind that prayer works. And the thing is, that's not a rare or unusual story. God – the all-powerful Creator of the universe, seems to choose to intervene in the tiniest parts of our lives when we invite and ask him to; the problem is, we just don't ask very often. Over the course of my life, I've seen this kind of 'coincidence' happen again and again. It's one of the surest reasons I have to believe that this God is real.

9 ***What the disciples did next.*** You might have heard about the 12 disciples of Jesus – the men who followed him around for three years, before being left to set up the foundations of the Church as we know it today. Maybe we're not so familiar with the end of the story – so let me fill it in for you. After Judas betrayed Jesus, he was understandably ejected from the group and replaced by a guy named Matthias, who must have been a sort of best runner-up among all Jesus' other followers. Jesus ascended into heaven, and the Twelve then started travelling around, telling people his story. The various powers in the world at that time – mainly the Romans, but also the rulers of the few parts that empire hadn't

> conquered – didn't take kindly to the Christian message of submission to a greater God. So one by one, these men were executed – some of them in torturous ways: crucifixion, stoning, burning. In each case, all they needed to do to preserve their own lives was to admit that the whole resurrection-of-Jesus thing was a lie; but in every case they didn't. Why would men die for a lie? Answer: they wouldn't – and because of their willingness to give everything for what they believed, thousands of people joined their little religion. Over the centuries, during which the Roman Empire itself converted to Christianity, those thousands became millions, and today, billions. All because that original group knew that what they'd seen was real.

Here's my point: any one of these reasons alone provides a good *argument* for believing in the Christian God. Left on their own, though, they're open to niggling doubt; the thought that perhaps coincidence is a better explanation. Put them all on top of each other, and it all becomes compelling. It's not just that I think I've seen and experienced the power of God; it's not just that I've seen him at work in other people; it's not just that it makes logical sense; it's all of these things and more that makes me believe that God is real, that the Bible is true and that the claims of the Christian faith really are worth listening to.

Now you've got a choice to make. As my old hero C. S. Lewis said: 'Christianity, if false, is of no importance, and if true, of infinite importance. The only thing it cannot be is moderately important.'

If by this point you're joining me on the 'convinced' side of the line, you can't just smile and shrug. If the Creator of the entire universe is real *and* wants to know you, then once you've truly realized that, you can't simply do nothing. That would be like finding a pile of bank notes in the street and not even picking it up. Doing nothing is crazy at this point.

So here's a very practical thing we can do: we can say 'yes' to God. If we believe he's real, we believe he's good and we believe he really is the Almighty, then we can join the billions who've gone before us and say, 'God, I want to follow and serve you.'

At this stage, then, it's worth diving quickly into the key points of the Christian faith, just so you're sure you know what the deal is. Here's a brief overview:

- God made humankind for relationship with him, but humans rebelled. Whether that means Adam and Eve, or the way that all of us decide to be selfish and ignore him, it's true, and we're all at fault. The broken relationship meant that people would die at the end of their lives, instead of living with God for ever.

- However, despite the rebellion, God still loves us. He sent his Son Jesus to earth. Jesus lived a perfect life and so was the only person in history who, by God's rules, didn't actually deserve to die.

- Jesus then said (in a manner of speaking): even though I'm perfect, I'll die, which breaks the whole deserving-death system. And he did – on Good Friday, on the cross.

- By dying, he took all the blame for everyone else's rebellion against God, and restored the relationship between heaven and earth. This also meant that those who believed in him and invested in this fixed relationship would get to live for ever. Like, genuinely – for ever, in paradise, with no pain or bad stuff.

- As Jesus was God, he was too powerful to stay dead, and so he came back to life after a couple of days: his resurrection – a historically verified event – helps to prove who he was.

- Now, Jesus is alive in heaven with God, and he's present in the world through the Holy Spirit. He is not distant but close by; he wants a friendship with us, and he has stuff for us to do, because . . .

- God is slowly remaking the world – his 'kingdom' is breaking into the earth. And eventually there will be a moment when the scales tip, Jesus returns, and earth becomes transformed into an eternal place of perfection.

Those are the very basics you need to know before making an informed decision. Because the next question is: do you want in? Do you want to say, 'I'm sorry that I've lived without seeing the bigger picture, and that I've focused on myself more than others'? Do you want to have a personal friendship with the most magnificent person in the history of the universe? Do you want access to unbelievable power and the chance to be part of a revolutionary movement of love and kindness that will literally transform the world until there is no more evil, no more crying, no more pain?

If you *do*, then for heaven's sake tell him now, for the first time or for the twenty-first: I want in. If you find this sort of thing tricky, here's a simple prayer you could read off the page now:

> God – I believe you're real.
> I'm sorry for the times I've ignored you or said you're not there.
> I'm sorry for the ways I've hurt other people, myself and you.
> I want to be part of your family, and your plan to rescue the world.
> If it's all or nothing, I'm all in.

It's as simple as that. If you've just prayed that prayer, then while nothing massive might have happened here on earth, there was just a small party in heaven. Maybe not even a small one; because God loves you more than you can possibly know. Is it not a mind-exploding thought, that the guy who orchestrates the entire universe is currently smiling because of you?

That decision – to choose all over nothing – is the greatest, most important and significant decision you could ever make. The rest of your life is now subject to all kinds of change and adventure. From this point forward, you can never again be truly alone; from this moment on, you are part of the solution to the world's greatest needs. What an incredible thing.

If you have just prayed those words, perhaps for the first time in your life, please don't leave it there. Call a friend who also believes in Jesus, or get in touch with someone from your local church. Sometimes the brilliant clarity that we have in a defining moment like this can fade a bit when the usual mix of mobile notifications and trending Netflix shows rushes in to distract us. So, seriously – please – put the book down and tell someone, right now.

The rest of this book is devoted to exploring what it means to live your life from now on in the light of that decision. It's about asking, 'If I'm now going to live a Christian life, then what kind of life is that?' You may imagine that it involves lots of sitting and listening to boring people, wearing unfashionable clothes and singing weird songs. So here's the good news – it doesn't *necessarily* have to mean those things. Because those aren't the hallmarks of adventure, of being one of the good guys; of changing the world. If those things are what Christianity has become then it's time to think again.

If we are God's children, reconnected to him thanks to Jesus, and a part of his master plan to save the world, then we're not his passive subjects. We're not sitting here waiting for him to decide when it's judgement day; we're on a mission with him, ready and able to work alongside him. He's at the centre of all things, and our lives are spent in dynamic relationship with him.

You see, we're in his orbit . . .

We are satellites.

2.

ORBIT

I'm a film buff. I love movies, and I've seen way more of them than is probably normal. If I ever get a chance to go on a long-distance flight, I like to see how many films I can cram in over the duration of the journey. Films enable us to feel and see things that otherwise might seem out of reach, and they give us reference points for our everyday lives. I'm certain at some point you've had an experience and thought, 'That's *just like* that bit in *Paper Towns/Paddington 2/ Die Hard.*'*

**All right, hopefully not* Die Hard, *for at least two reasons.*

Anyway, forgive me for calling on a cinematic reference that might be unfamiliar, but I don't want to patronize you by just comparing everything to a Marvel movie (at least, not until Chapter 6). So: at some point we all feel like Truman.

If you've never seen the classic 1998 film, *The Truman Show* tells the story of a man played by Jim Carrey, who feels as if the world revolves around him. In most cases you'd think that was a sign of extreme self-centredness, but in Truman's case it's actually true. It turns out that his entire life is one giant TV show – since birth he's been living inside an artificially created world, his every move tracked by television cameras and broadcast across America. Every person he interacts with is played by an actor, and a cast and crew of thousands are employed around him to ensure two things: that his life remains interesting enough to keep ratings up, and that he never works out that there's a whole world out there beyond the one he knows.

This sort of idea crosses a lot of people's minds at some point growing up. What if it *is* all about me? What if *I am* the most important person in the universe – and everyone else is simply here to play a secondary character?

Even if that thought has never occurred to you, the truth is that this is exactly how most of us instinctively tend to live our lives. We naturally make our decisions based on what's good for us first, and then how others are affected second. If there's one slice of pizza left and we're hungry, then there's a strong urge to take it; if someone asks us for some money, and giving it to them would leave us short, we tend to say an apologetic 'no'. These are hardly criminal acts, but there's no doubt that our instinct is to look after ourselves before we consider others. Perhaps that just feels like common sense.

You're probably not a huge conspiracy theorist who believes that they're trapped in a giant TV show, but it's very likely that you are the centre of your own world. What I mean is that you have aspirations for your life, and ultimately they all come back to benefit you. Perhaps you're at the stage where your hopes and dreams extend only as far as eating well and playing as many hours of video games as you can. Or maybe you're starting to dream a bit bigger – for a family of your own, a good job, nice car and your own home. Or you might have a really huge dream: like becoming a successful entrepreneur, or YouTuber, or actor – or maybe even being one of those annoying people who manages to do all those things at once. Whatever your dreams, it's likely – natural even – that they all stem from you; all place you at the centre of the world, living the best life possible and squeezing every last drop of enjoyment out of the journey. This is the life that calls to you, and has been calling to you since the first time someone tried to sell you a toddler toy through a television advert. You can have it all; it's all about *you*.

In many ways, we're all living in our own personalized version of *The Truman Show*.

When you're at the centre of your world, everything revolves around you. You figure out what's right for you, which choices are most likely to get you to where you want to go in life and make you happy in the short or long term, and you follow that path. Everything else, and to some extent every*one* else, serves that purpose. You hang out with the friends who make you feel happy; you accumulate stuff – clothes, technology, food – as you need it, and you throw it away when it breaks or spoils. Now, let's not be naive: there are some benefits to living that way. You get to experience a fair amount of pleasure and fun. You tend not to go hungry, or without shelter or comfort. You probably laugh a lot and you mostly get your own way. Selfishness is not without merits.

However, there are also some major downsides. For a start, it's not great news for any of the other people in your life, who naturally get treated as second-class citizens. When you're at the centre of your world, everyone else ultimately exists to serve you – just like Truman. But there's also another, more personal, reason why self-centredness doesn't work: you probably never get to experience true happiness that way. I'm not talking about momentary pleasure here: punching the air because your sports team won or taking the first bite into a slice of Red Velvet cake.* I mean that deep feeling of rightness in the depth of your being: contentment. Humans don't get to feel deeply fulfilled when they think only about themselves.

**The undisputed king of all cakes.*

I suppose the natural opposite to this might be to put other people at the centre of our world. That might even feel like classic Christian teaching – after all, Jesus makes a pretty big deal of loving one another (John 15.12). Yet, while it certainly seems more noble than option one, it also has a pretty massive flaw: people let you down. We can't help it – we do it to other people, and they in turn disappoint us. Just ask the devoted husband who dedicated 20 years of his life to making his wife happy, only to discover a letter on the kitchen table telling him she'd run off with the builder. Just ask the schoolteacher who invested three decades of her career in educating the next generation, before repeated changes in government policy turned the job she loved into nothing more than a series of soul-crushing attainment tests. Even putting other people at the centre of our lives doesn't lead to ultimate fulfilment. At least, that alone can't do it.

You will not be shocked to see where I'm going here. Of course, I believe the best thing you could put at the centre of your life – the best person in fact – is God. You are probably rolling your eyes at the very obviousness of it. But give me a chance; let me explain.

If the God described by the Christian faith is real – and if you've made it this far you're probably fairly sure he is – then not only is he the most important thing in the universe, but what he says about himself is true. Here's something Jesus says in the Gospel of John – one of the books written about his life on earth: 'I have come that they may have life, and have it to the full' (John 10.10b).

The 'they' described here are people who follow Jesus. He promises (and when he makes promises, he always keeps them) that his followers will experience life *to the full*. Another group of people who translated the Bible from its original language put it like this: 'they may have life *in all its fullness*' – as if people who follow Jesus are able to squeeze every last drop of juicy goodness out of being alive. And yet another translator (in a paraphrase of the Bible called

The Message) puts it like this: 'I came so they can have real and eternal life, more and better life than they ever dreamed of.'

More and better life than they ever dreamed of. That's what Jesus offers to his followers. And not only the greatest possible experience of life for the years they spend on earth, but *for ever.*

This is a really important point. So important that, if this was a film, the soundtrack music would have suddenly changed and there would have been a close-up of my face as I said it in an emotionally charged voice. The incredible experience of life that Jesus offers to those who follow him is both for now and then for the life that we experience after we die: eternity.

It's easy to fall into one of two traps at this point. Either you think the point of following Jesus is about passing the exam to get into heaven, or you focus entirely on the present and act as if eternity is a nice, metaphorical idea. But both are true – Jesus wants us to live life to the fullest possible potential while we're alive, and then experience the extraordinary reality of an everlasting life with him after we die.

On paper, this sounds like the sweetest deal since Oprah Winfrey gave away US$7.7 million of free cars.* Following Jesus gives you the best possible life *and* the promise that you get to live for ever. In fact, it gets even better.

**You know the thing. YOU GET A CAR! YOU GET A CAR! No? Have you been living on Pluto?*

The last section of the Bible is – I'm not going to lie to you – pretty weird. The book of Revelation is basically a transcript of a vision given to Jesus' last surviving disciple (John) while he was enjoying his retirement on the Greek island of Patmos. In this vision there are monsters, plagues, freaky horse-locusts, and a pregnant woman fighting a dragon (and, to be honest, who hasn't had *that* dream?). But then at the very end of all that, there's an incredibly important promise: that God will make everything right again; that, ultimately, good will win out over evil.

Revelation feels like a pretty relevant book right now. As I write these words in early 2020, I am sitting in an enforced lockdown at home while pretty much every country on earth is trying to figure out how to stop the spread of the Covid-19 virus. This disease has tragically caused so many deaths, has had an impact on all sorts of things about our way of life that we took for granted, and will almost certainly cause major ripples that will last for years. And even putting the virus to one side, the world is facing all sorts of problems. Environmental catastrophe continues to loom, and several nations around the world are either locked in terrible conflict or skirting close to the beginnings of war. We may not be facing horse-sized locusts, but the monsters are all too real. Thank God then – and I mean that literally – that this vision in Revelation gives us the most amazing hope:

> Then I saw 'a new heaven and a new earth,' for the first heaven and the first earth had passed away, and there was no longer any sea. I saw the Holy City, the new Jerusalem, coming down out of heaven from God, prepared as a bride beautifully dressed for her husband. And I heard a loud voice from the throne saying, 'Look! God's dwelling-place is now among the people, and he will dwell with them. They will be his people, and God himself will be with them and be their God. "He will wipe every tear from their eyes. There will be no more death" or mourning or crying or pain, for the old order of things has passed away.'
>
> He who was seated on the throne said, 'I am making everything new!' Then he said, 'Write this down, for these words are trustworthy and true.'

> He said to me: 'It is done. I am the Alpha and the Omega, the Beginning and the End. To the thirsty I will give water without cost from the spring of the water of life.'
> (Revelation 21.1–6)

This is the moment that everything leads to. Think of your favourite epic film series – *Star Wars*, *Harry Potter*, the MCU – this is the part after the final battle, when the light finally overwhelms the darkness despite almost overwhelming odds. All the monsters finally get defeated and God himself takes the throne. There's no more death, no more grief, no more tears – and what's more everything that was broken gets completely renewed. It's the ultimate redemption, and it's not just a story. It's what God says will really happen at the end of life as we know it. There will be a moment in history where this actually happens. I don't know about you, but I find that pretty comforting.

So, if that's the offer – the best possible life now *and* the perfect, painless, everlasting life to come – where do we sign?

Well, here's the even better part. There's nothing we have to do in order to be part of God's in-crowd. There are no hoops to jump through or levels of attainment to achieve. The only thing we really have to do is put our faith in him. In fact, if you were able to agree along with that prayer in the last chapter then there's really nothing else you *need* to do. If you've invited Jesus to be a part of your life, he will be.

Having said that . . . while there's nothing you can do to earn God's love for you, or his offer of eternal life, it would seem pretty crazy at this point to do nothing at all. Because if he really does offer the fullest, best experience of life on earth, surely it's a good idea to look into what he says that looks like.

People in the Bible wonder similar things. One day, Jesus was asked a simple question by the religious leaders: 'What is the greatest commandment?' What they were really asking was, 'What is the most important rule for the way I live my life?' Jesus, who was rather clever when it came to answering religious people, gave not one response but two:

> Jesus replied: '"Love the Lord your God with all your heart and with all your soul and with all your mind." This is the first and greatest commandment. And the second is like it: "Love your neighbour as yourself." All the Law and the Prophets hang on these two commandments.'
> (Matthew 22.37–40)

For Jesus, these two things were inseparable: love God with everything you have, and love other people. In fact, the clearest way that you can express that you love God, and want to follow in his ways, is to do these two things. Practically, that is what it looks like **to place God at the centre of your world**. It's what we were made for.

*

When you place something at the centre of your world, everything else kind of revolves around it. For example: I know a family in which the son is a precociously talented young footballer. He's been invited to train regularly with a Premier League team that plays about 40 minutes from his home. His family dutifully drive him there and back again on two nights of each week. He's also been invited to train with a second team, much further away, on another night each week; recently he's accepted an invitation to spend yet another night with a third. Weekends are reserved for matches. He's eight years old.

Such is his family's determination to give him a shot at Premier League stardom, they have orientated their whole lives around his footballing ambitions. They're sacrificing any thought of a social life, and investing thousands of pounds in fuel, because their twinkle-toed child *might* make it in the UK's most competitive sport. His football training is at the centre of their lives, and everything else – every decision and every other commitment – orbits around it. Football is the centre and everything else comes second.

Another friend has become a fierce environmentalist and 'green' campaigner. She's so concerned by the climate crisis that she does everything within her power to lessen her contribution to it. She not only recycles everything but steers away from single-use plastic in the way that most of us would evade a hungry lion. She eats no meat, refuses to fly unless it is absolutely essential, and she carbon-offsets every car journey she makes. Not only that, but she works hard to encourage others to adopt everything from fair trade to vegetarianism. Every decision she makes serves the passion that sits at the centre of her life.

There are worse things to put at the heart of your life than a concern for the environment or an unswerving commitment to your sport. Yet does either, alone, truly offer *life in all its fullness?* I don't think so.

Jesus has another famous catchphrase, found in John 14.6. He said, 'I am the way and the truth and the life.' It's another way of saying that he is the only person worth putting at the very epicentre of your world. He's 'the life' – the very best version of it, and the only version that goes on for ever. So what does that life look like? What does it mean to experience 'the life' that Jesus describes?

I should probably make this clear: Jesus offering the best version of life does not necessarily mean that life with Jesus will be *easy.*

Sometimes, following him will mean making difficult and unpopular decisions, saying 'no' to something that we really want to do or losing out on something ourselves for the sake of someone else. There's a cost to loving God and other people – but even that cost is all part of living the best life possible.

I don't believe that the life we experience happens by chance but rather that we're made as tiny but vital pieces of one enormous cosmic machine. I think we're created – *designed* even – by a designer who makes the best guys at Apple look like kids in their first year at school. And he's offered all of those moving parts a choice: to be part of the whole, or ignore it; even to work against it if we want to. So we can choose not to play a part in this grand story – and if we do, the machine will continue to work – but we can make another choice: to say 'yes' to our Creator, and live our lives as willing participants in his plan.

In many ways, the part we're created to play is different for everyone. We're all unique, and so are the ways in which we will spend our lives. But in another way, we're all made to be the same *kind* of part in that metaphorical machine. We're created to orbit and orientate our lives around the God who lies at the centre of it all. I think a really good way to describe the life that Jesus offers, and the way in which we relate to God, is the image of a satellite.

Did you know that, at the time of writing, there are 4,994 satellites orbiting Earth? To be fair, why *would* you know that? Even I had to look it up. Each one of them is there for a reason, launched from Earth for the purposes of communication, space exploration, weather monitoring and, of course, top-secret military stuff. But none of those purposes would make sense if it weren't for the thing they're actually orbiting: Earth. Without that, they're just expensive bits of metal, flying in a circle.

In the same way, we're all created for a purpose, launched into the universe with different abilities and roles to play – but ultimately none of that makes sense unless we recognize the place from which we were launched; unless we know who made us and why.

Orbit is probably the first and most important attribute for a satellite. If it continues to orbit Earth, then it can keep doing the job that it was made for. If it hits a bit of space debris or another satellite, it goes spinning out of that orbit, loses contact with the Earth, and ends up floating alone for ever through deep space. If the satellite maintains clear contact with Earth, it can continue to function, and if it does that, then we can think about the second major attribute of most satellites: they're made to broadcast and to receive.

Let me explain: a spy satellite isn't hugely useful if it receives instructions to take lots of pictures over enemy territory, does so and then never sends them home. A TV satellite is completely useless if it just receives the pictures beamed to it from Earth and then simply stores them away in its memory banks. The reverse is also true – phone satellites can't generate their own conversations. No, satellites only work if there's a balance between what goes in and what comes out.

Orbiting our lives around God involves achieving the same kind of balance. In and out; receive and broadcast. The Christian life – *life in all its fullness* – is best lived in exactly this way: in close orbit of our God, receiving from him and then doing the work he created us for. The rest of this book will explore what it means to do each of these things, and how, somehow, miraculously, he becomes involved in all of it to give us the very greatest experience of life imaginable.

But before we move on: you remember earlier on I suggested that putting other people at the centre of your world isn't ultimately the best idea? Well, what I actually said was that doing that *alone* wouldn't give you the most fulfilling version of life. However, since Jesus' own rules for living well were number 1 love God, and number 2 love one another, putting other people first is clearly very close to the top of the agenda. Once we put God at the centre of our lives, he naturally leads us to then put other people before ourselves.

Which would seem like bad news for the Trumans of this world – the people who are living at the heart of their own imaginary TV show, where everything revolves around them. But wait: there's something really clever going on. If everyone in the world was functioning in their proper place, orbiting around God and putting others first as a result, the only person not putting you first . . . would be you! Isn't that amazing? In God's great system, this plan for remaking the world, wiping every tear and making everything new, everyone gets prioritized and taken care of. There's no way the energy that you could expend on loving yourself could ever be a match for every person around you looking out for you and looking after you. That's why putting yourself at the heart of your world makes no sense; it's simply no match for what God has had planned for you all along.

*

That's the foundations covered: God is real, wants a relationship with you and offers you the best and fullest life imaginable, with him at the centre of it. That's the big idea; that's why this book has, let's just be honest, a slightly weird title.

The other seven chapters take us through the values and practices of the Christian faith in a bit more detail. Or, to put that another way, they explain what living as a follower of Jesus can look like *in practice*. And (at the risk of stretching our metaphor too far) we can also view these seven aspects in the light of how a satellite works.

First, we'll look at three elements of following Jesus that are about us. Input – the stuff that we do that helps us to get closer to, and perhaps become a bit more like, Jesus. Like a satellite needs to receive a signal before broadcasting it, this is our 'receiving' bit. We'll look at **prayer**, and what it means to have a relationship with God (because, honestly, that sounds very strange when you say it out loud), and we'll try to understand what we mean by **worship** – and not just singing songs, but how we choose to live everyday life. Then we'll see why God has called us to be part of a **family**, the Church.

The final three chapters will look at the other side of the equation; let's call it the 'output'. In this section, we'll look at the elements of the Christian faith that are about us getting involved in God's world; rolling our sleeves up and getting our hands dirty alongside him as he seeks to sort out this mess. We'll talk about **justice**, and how God cares so deeply about those who don't have it. We'll look at **evangelism**, and why it's important that we share our faith with other people. Finally, we'll talk about our God-given **creativity**, and what it means to put it to use in remaking and repainting the world.

Which makes six, and I clearly said seven. The last element – or should I say person? – sits in the middle of those two sections. We'll also explore the **power** of the Holy Spirit, which flows through every single one of those things. The Spirit is part of the input (us being formed as followers of Jesus) and the output (the work God has for us to do in the world).

Eager beavers might notice that this list doesn't include a separate chapter on the Bible. This is not because I don't think it's an important or central part of being a Christian. It is – and reading the Bible regularly is one of the most important things you can do if you want to develop a strong faith.

However, *everything* in this book sits on the things that we learn about God in the Bible, and you'll see me quoting from it often. If we were making a list of important tools for living as a Christian, the Bible would be number one. What follows, however, are seven elements of what it means to follow Jesus, *based entirely* on the Bible.

My hope is that what you read in the rest of this book will inspire you to place God at the centre of your world, inviting him into every element of your life. You are stepping into the way that things were always meant to be: a life designed by the Creator of the entire universe. I think that's a pretty exciting place to find yourself.

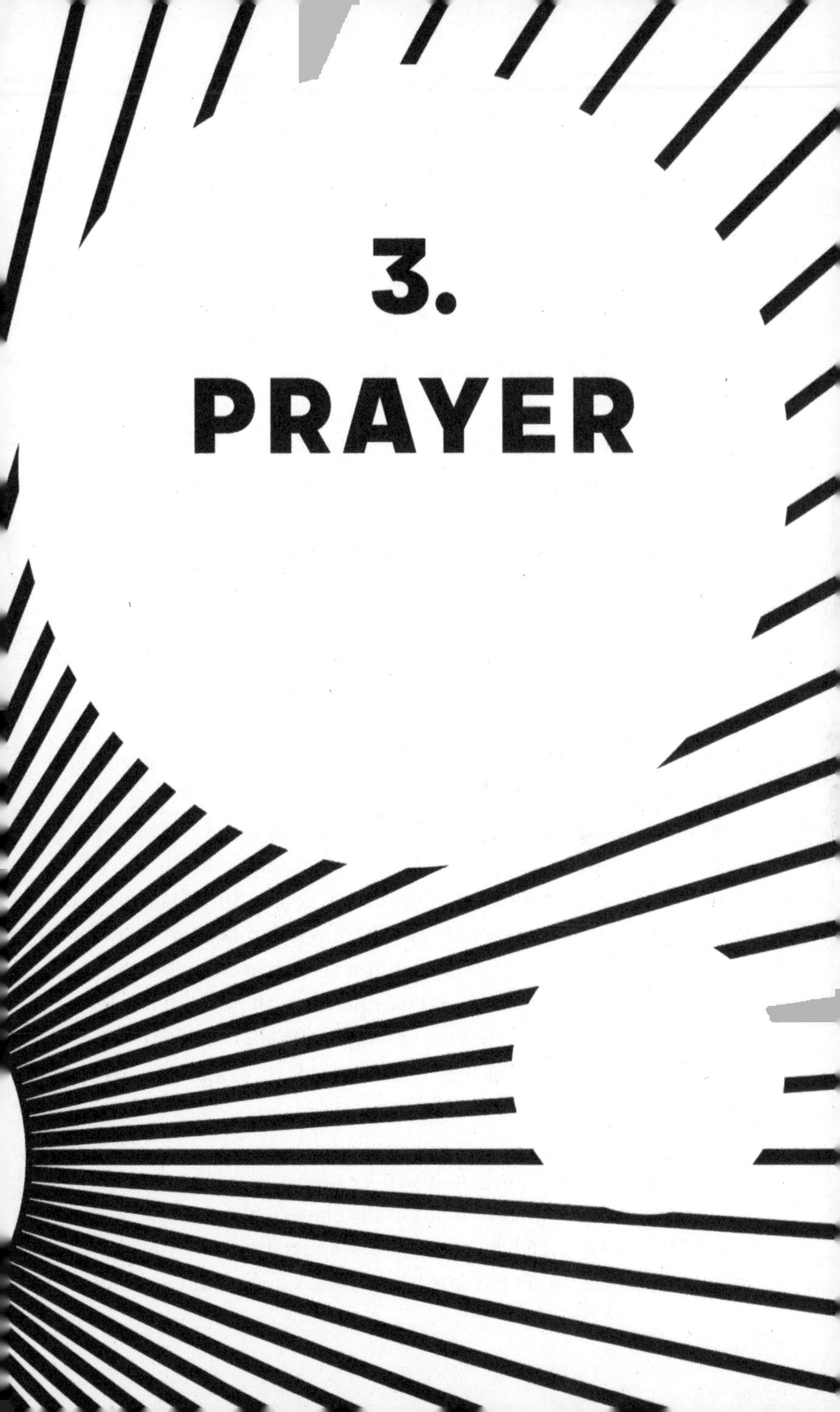

3.

PRAYER

You're on a plane, let's say halfway across the Atlantic Ocean. You've managed to make yourself fairly comfortable, despite sitting behind one of those monstrous people who subtly keep reclining their seat until it's gone back as far as possible. You're midway through a moderately entertaining in-flight film, and because it's only recently been in cinemas you feel as though you're winning. The meal was not awful and the flight appears to be making good time. Things are going well.

Suddenly you hear a strange clunking noise and everyone around you starts to look concerned. Over the intercom, the captain announces some sort of special code to his crew and the seatbelt sign quickly flashes on. Much more worryingly, the cabin crew start moving frantically around the cabin, demanding that people get back in their seats. They always say that if you want to know if you should be concerned, you should just look at the cabin crew, because even in gravity-defying circumstances they'll still be gliding serenely around, serving tea and coffee. Well, they've all gone white as sheets, and soon they've all run off to strap themselves in too.

Then there's another clunk, followed by silence. And then you feel your stomach turning somersaults as the plane begins to rapidly descend. Oxygen masks fall from above, and you're suddenly filled with remorse that you didn't pay attention to the safety demonstration.

So, as the plane freefalls and everyone else around you starts to lose their heads, what do you do? When the situation seems totally desperate, completely impossible, what is your last resort?

I think most of us would pray.

Whether it was a daily habit or something we'd never even contemplated, in those circumstances reaching out to a higher power would probably feel like the last card any of us had left to play. We'd call out to God because whatever belief we had in our ability to navigate life without him would now have evaporated; we would now have zero confidence in our chances of saving ourselves. We'd need a miracle, and even the most self-assured person doesn't believe they can generate those.

(If you're reading this on a plane, by the way, apologies. I should probably point out that statistically you were much more likely to be involved in a deadly incident on your way to the airport. You weren't, so relax – things are going great!)

If your plane *was* going down, though, I think you'd have to be a pretty hardened atheist not to whisper a few words, just in case. What other hope would you have?

Now, let's imagine that straight after you've spoken those words, 'God, save me', into the otherwise-scream-filled air, the situation suddenly begins to improve dramatically. The plane levels out, the engines whirr and a relieved-sounding captain makes a second, much calmer announcement to his frazzled crew. Your life no longer flashing before your eyes, you would now surely find it impossible to detach the miraculous escape that appears to be occurring from the prayer that you just uttered. Your last resort has triggered the saving power of God, and faced with the realization not only of the reality of God but also his interest in your everyday welfare, you'd surely be asking yourself: why wasn't this my *first* resort? Why didn't I try praying years ago?

*

Depending on where and how you grew up, the word 'prayer' might have all sorts of connotations. You might associate it with being dragged to church, or with comforting family mealtimes. You could have experienced long, dull prayer meetings, where various people droned on in their attempts to both beseech the Almighty and impress their friends with flowery poetic language. Or you may have been taught to pray outdoors in the wild, on long conversational walks with the dog.*

**As in, you'd be talking to God while walking the dog. Although, to be totally honest, I talk to my dog when we're out walking, and while I don't believe she has the power to help me solve some of my major life issues, she does at least fetch a ball when I ask her to.*

Whatever your experience of prayer, though, it's highly likely that you imagine it's more complicated than it really is. Over the years Christians have created all these formulae and styles of prayer, and added in all this wizardy language that can often make outsiders feel as though they need to take a class before they can even attempt it. But here's the truth: prayer is simply you and God, in conversation. *That's it.* It's just you, talking with God.

My son Zachary is six, and as talkative as Donkey from *Shrek*. A few weeks ago, he and I went to see the greatest football team in the world, West Ham United.* It is no exaggeration to say that Zachary did not stop talking for the entirety of that trip. He talked about trains, and then London, as we made our way to the city; he asked questions about the stadium as we approached and entered it; he gave a full commentary on the match and analysed it all the way home. At times I talked too, but most of the way I was just listening.

**Not objectively true.*

Here's the first thing to say: at no point during that day did I stop Zachary to correct his use of words, or instruct him to address me as his father in more formal language. I tried not to interrupt him, and I made myself available to him all day. I let him guide the conversation, and I chipped in when I had something to add. Here's the second thing: *I absolutely loved it.* Listening to him share what was on his mind; laughing at his little jokes, and watching him implore the manager to substitute-off an underperforming Ukrainian named Andriy Yarmolenko – all of it was joy for me. Of course it was – I'm his dad; I love him (and my other kids) in a way that I didn't even imagine was possible until I met him. My experience of our conversations that day was as good as life gets.

I think that's a pretty good picture of what prayer is meant to be like. God doesn't need our clever language; he doesn't need us to be in a special place or position, or with special people, in order to access him. He just wants our conversation – in fact, incredibly, he desires the joy of it in the same way I love chatting with my kids. Of course he does: he's our Father, our Maker and our ultimate *Dad.*

Much like that conversation between my six-year-old and me, prayer often involves us doing most of the talking. But not all of it. If we stop to listen, we also discover that God talks back. Sometimes that's through an action – something happening or changing around us as we talk to him, like the story I shared earlier on about my son and the loud woman in the supermarket. More often it's a kind of thought-voice that we hear in among the other ideas that are floating around our minds – a kind of alien whisper that we know hasn't come from us. And sometimes, just sometimes, it actually can be an audible voice – like a person speaking to us.

I am aware that's a pretty out-there thing to say. When I was at school, I distinctly remember that the people who didn't share my Christian faith said that the first sign of madness is talking to yourself, and the second sign is thinking you've heard a reply. Yet I can't deny that on three occasions in my life (and only three, which in over 40 years really isn't that many), I believe I've heard God actually speak to me, out loud. I don't want to make this weirder, but I was naked two of those times.

Let me give you an example of one of them. I was in a hotel room in Dallas, Texas. I'd been away from home for a few days at a conference, and the plan was to fly on to Los Angeles for a meeting with a Hollywood producer, who was interested in buying the film rights to a terrible novel I had written.* My wife was at home, working, and we didn't have children at the time. On the final morning of the conference, I woke up with a start, and after a few seconds of being awake I heard a voice saying simply: 'Go home to your wife.' That was it. No profound spiritual words; no important bits of life direction. Just a single instruction – and despite my utter desperation to get to LA and make it in the movies, I knew with total conviction that I had to obey. I got up, called the airline and got them to change everything. Miraculously, they did so without charge.

**Let me be the first to say that the fact that my football-based epic* England's Messiah *never made it to the Big Screen is a loss to nobody. It's also possible that this 'Hollywood producer' was actually a serial killer.*

When I got home, I had absolute certainty that I had done the right thing. My wife, who hadn't told me over the phone that she was going through an incredibly tough time, simply could not believe her eyes when she saw me on the doorstep 16 hours later. God had spoken and thankfully I'd listened.

That isn't always how God speaks – you're certainly not weird or exceptional if you never hear God in that way – but it is how he *can*, if he wants to. The truth is that, since he's God, he can choose to speak to us in all manner of ways. We just need to be alive and alert to the fact that if we talk to God, he might just reply. Because he's our heavenly Dad – why on earth wouldn't he?

What he desires is that conversation, that relationship with us. In a way that probably sounds slightly strange and irritating if you're not a parent. I crave those long conversations with Zachary because I love him deep in the very core of my being. His words light me up. The sense of our relationship growing and deepening feels incredibly profound. That's how it is for God when we talk and spend time with him, because he's not some far-off abstract deity; he's a father who wants to know his children.

*

My early teenage years came before the widespread introduction of the internet. There were no smartphones or online games; we had to stand around outside in the freezing cold if we wanted to hang out with our friends, and if we wanted to rent a movie, we had to walk down to a video shop and choose one.* Then, one day, when I was around 16 or 17 years old, my parents made the jump into the digital world. Each of us was issued with an AOL email address, and my dad walked us through the intricacies of what was then called 'logging on'.

**Blockbuster Video was one of the best and we would regularly spend the entire evening trying to choose between films, rather than* *actually watching them (as we still do). It was basically like standing inside a physical version of Netflix.*

Back then, the internet came through the same line as your home phone – which was wired in somewhere downstairs. It was called 'dial-up' internet, and that meant that if you wanted to go online you literally had to call the internet on your telephone. The obvious implication, since dial-up internet made a high-pitch screeching that sounded like R2D2 being tortured, was that you couldn't do that *and* make an actual phone call at the same time (I know, sounds barbaric, right?). So you had to ask your parents if you wanted to log on and check your email, or visit one of the world's 12 half-decent websites. And if your parents forgot, as my mum constantly did, she'd pick up the phone to a five-second burst of screaming droid-torture, and the connection would be lost.

Today, the internet is accessible almost everywhere through smartphones – or at least until your data runs out* – and within your home it's generally available without limit, at superfast speeds, and instantly. You don't have to 'log on', because you're always connected. If you want to check your social media accounts, or ask Siri who fought at the Battle of Hastings, you can do so with no delay, as if the whole world's library of information and your entire friendship circle were present right there with you in the lavatory.

**I like to think that in 20 years' time, someone might pick up this book, read about 'running out of data' and scoff, 'How primitive!' in much the same way my kids now laugh that I used to walk around with a portable cassette player clipped to my belt.*

I think the difference between how we now access the internet and how we did so a couple of decades ago is a good metaphor for how we can think about prayer. For a whole range of reasons, most of us tend to treat praying a bit like sitting down to 'dial up' the internet. It's something we think we have to make a specific time and space for; something that's finished after we log off with an 'amen', and that can be left incomplete if someone walks in halfway through.

In the Bible, though, Paul, one of the main authors of the New Testament, says that we should 'pray continually' (1 Thessalonians 5.17), or, in another translation, 'pray without ceasing'. By this, I do not imagine he means that life should look like the following scenario:

> I enter the supermarket, thanking God for his goodness and his provision. I turn left into chilled food, and ask for guidance: should I first meet my need for milk, or for cheese? Feeling drawn to the cheese, I seek the Lord earnestly for the right maturity of cheddar, and contemplate quietly whether I should purchase the slab, pre-sliced or grated option. After making my decision, I turn to the milk and sing a song of worship to God for his glorious invention: the cow. Thanking him for farmers, and asking his forgiveness for my use of plastic bottles, I pick up four pints and make my way towards the many choices of the ham aisle.

I mean, there would be nothing wrong with that, but you might struggle to get through your weekly shop before it was time to do the next one. I think what Paul actually means when he says we should 'pray continually' is to see prayer as a four bars of wi-fi signal, an always-on kind of arrangement. And unlike phone data, which can occasionally get a bit patchy in valleyed areas, God's reception is always perfect. There is literally no limit to where and when we can pray, or where and when we can hear from him.

So if you're standing on the football field, struggling against a fearsome or cheating opponent, you have instant access to God through prayer. If you're up alone at night, overwhelmed with fear or anxiety, you have that same access. If you're in the middle of a science exam where suddenly nothing you're reading seems to make any sense; if you're at a party and you think you're about to make a bad decision; if you're caught up in an awkward online conversation; if you're celebrating; if you've just done the worst thing you've ever done . . . in any or all of those situations, you can call out to God in prayer and he will instantly hear you. You don't have to dial him up; he's there, alongside you, every moment of your life, every step of the way.

Prayer is the most impossibly real function of being a human: the actual ability for one tiny person to talk directly to the God who made and sustains the entire universe. It's like a superpower, when you stop to think about it.

*

Prayer is practising the presence of God. Have you ever bought something that required practice in order for you to get the most out of it? Like a musical instrument, or a complex game, or maybe a book that promised to teach you a new skill or even a new language?

When I was about 13, I asked my parents if I could learn to play the clarinet. I don't know why I chose that instrument; it seems so unglamorous that I can only assume I was trying desperately to stand out and be different from all the cool guitarists and drummers. Perhaps I had visions of joining a school band that played covers of popular songs with a clarinet solo inserted! I don't know. Anyway, my kindly father bought a second-hand clarinet (we were not wealthy, and it was not cheap), and I excitedly began my tuition.

Or rather . . . I felt very proud of my clarinet. I don't know if you're familiar with them, but they've got loads of shiny bits that you can polish. They are, however, pretty hard to play, and even practising – especially in the early days – is hard work. Lessons are also fairly gruelling; you've got to learn the really simple stuff first, which means hours of trying to understand how to blow into a funny little reed thing. So while I did a lot of polishing and posing with my clarinet, I didn't really do a lot of practising. And because I didn't do much of that, I was too embarrassed to attend the lessons . . . so all I ever really qualified to do was hold a long black stick in my hand. My parents were not thrilled.

The clarinet was all mine, but because I didn't invest any time into it I missed out on the richness of being able to make music. And that's a little similar to the choice we have when it comes to our relationship with God. If we invite him to be a part of our lives, he will be; that's a promise. But if we never invest any time in practising – or being with him – then we're missing out on so much of what is available to us.

In a nutshell, that's why prayer – connection and communication with God – is one of the most important aspects of being a person whose life is in orbit around him. Perhaps it's the key value; the one that underpins all the others that we'll talk about in the coming pages.

*

Connection to God, or 'praying continually', is perhaps the most fundamental part of living as a follower of Jesus. It's the way in which we share our lives – our deepest heartaches and most profound joys – with the Creator of the universe who is somehow also our friend. It's a way of sharing everything that's bothering us with someone who will never stop listening; it's a rare opportunity for our hearts to express thankfulness for the good things in our lives. And, perhaps even more importantly, I believe that prayer changes situations.

I've been praying about the everyday stuff going on in my life for the last 25 years. I've prayed for small acts of help (like parking spaces); I've prayed for enormous and unlikely things. At the time, when these things went the way I was hoping, they often felt like welcome coincidences that *might* have been down to God. When I look back, however, at old journals, or at moments in my life that seemed desperate, I see those coincidences stack up and up on top of each other. Over and over again it seems either that I've got ridiculously lucky or that God has heard and responded to my prayers.

Now, I'm writing these words at pretty much the most difficult moment imaginable. A friend of mine was taken seriously ill a few days ago. He was rushed to hospital, and as news filtered back to my church of just how sick he was, the community rushed both to help practically and to pray. We gathered in the chapel hour after hour, for two days; people of all ages, close friends and people who'd never even met him. We called out to God with one voice – to heal and restore our friend, even though the medical evidence all suggested that recovery was impossible. And then he died. There was no miracle; his family was shattered and the church was left with all its hopeful prayers unanswered. He was my age.

Why didn't God intervene? Why didn't he hear our prayers? Why didn't he answer?

Much more intelligent people than me have been wrestling with that question since Christianity was born, and I'm certainly not going to be able to answer it comprehensively.

The painfully insubstantial answer is that this world is broken, and it is not our home. God's kingdom is real, and its influence is growing – but it is not dominant; it doesn't run the world. Ever see that bumper sticker/Instagram quote that 'God is in control'? Well here's the difficult truth: he isn't. Not on earth. On earth, for now, he has decided *not* to be in control. I realize that can be a bit unsettling to read.

God *is* on the throne in an eternal, universe-wide sense, but here he's chosen to give over the running of the world to us. Because he loves us too much to make us into robotic puppets, he gives us free choice; what theologians call **free will**. And while some of us choose to use that freedom to surrender to God and his kingdom, many don't. Others choose to use it to further their own fame or power or ideas about how the world should work. They choose things that are in direct conflict with the kingdom of God – like prejudice, war and hatred – or they just choose selfishness. As a result, we're living in a world where God *isn't* in control. We are. And a right mess of it we're making too.

Death and suffering are the terrible realities of a world run by us. The unvanquishable spark of light is that death is not the end. That promise of a new heaven and a new earth, where there's no more death or pain, is the reality of the world once it *is* run by God; the world we'll one day step into as followers of Jesus; the one my friend already now inhabits.

And yet, while God did not heal my friend, he does sometimes choose to heal others. At exactly the same time as the tragedy I've described was unfolding, my friend's nephew was being rushed to hospital with life-threatening symptoms. Again, many people prayed for him and, in this case, he made such a rapid and unexpected recovery that the doctors actually used the word 'miracle'. He's going to be fine.

Which throws up another question: why? Why would God spare one family the agony of death and force another to go right through it? At this point, I'm out of good answers. All I know is, the Bible says that 'in all things, God works for the good of those who love him' (Romans 8.28); and I believe that even includes tragedy.

God is not in control, but at all times, and in every situation, he *is* working, moving, bringing change. He *was* there comforting the family of my friend, even as they said goodbye to him. He *was* there in the community, as they processed their grief and felt inspired both to care for the family and to meaningfully mark his memory. He *will* be there in the years to come as that precious family continues to need support, comfort and peace, and in a very real way he *is* already there, standing alongside my friend in eternity.

And then here's the really tricky thing. As I was still grieving my friend, something incredible happened in another area of my life. I had been trying to raise money for about 18 months, in order to launch the summer youth event at which you might have even picked up this book. For the first 17 of those months, it was all a bit of a gruelling slog; I'd had to ask countless people if they'd consider supporting this idea – gathering a load of young people in a field to tell them about how Jesus can change the course of their lives – and I had to listen to the same answers over and over again. 'Sorry, it's not something we can get behind.' 'We wish you well, but we support lots of other things.' No, no, no.

Then suddenly, a few weeks ago, things started to change. One after another, people – many of whom I'd never met before – started queuing up to hand us money. The thing I'd been praying desperately for, that we'd somehow find the funds to launch this crazy dream, very quickly came to be. I can't go into the details, but trust me, the gifts and the speed in which they arrived were nothing short of miraculous. After months of famine, it was unexpectedly now feast time – like a sports team going on the worst run in their history and suddenly becoming world beaters.

I don't know why God would answer one prayer in a miraculous way and then seem to ignore another. Prayer can be frustrating sometimes. But that doesn't mean that it doesn't work; it doesn't mean we shouldn't do it. I guess the tough part of prayer is a bit like when you ask anyone for anything: the answer isn't always the one you're hoping for.

*

God isn't Santa. It's important to remember that when it comes to prayer. Because we're most naturally inclined to pray when we want or need something, we can often start to think about prayer in terms of 'presenting our requests to God'. And while that exact phrase does appear in the Bible (in Philippians 4.6), that's certainly not all prayer is. Asking for stuff is only a relatively small part of a good parent–child relationship. There's also the expression of gratitude for the things we've already received – saying thank you – and of course the ability to say sorry when we haven't behaved as we should.

While thank you, sorry and please are often listed as the building blocks of prayer, I think God desires something wider and more beautiful than that. He wants us to talk to him about everything; like we would to a parent who also just happened to be our best friend.

I think God wants to hear about the most boring intricacies of our day: our school lessons and our jobs; our sports teams and our nights out with friends. He wants to know when we're feeling lonely or insecure, or when everything feels right with the world. He's interested – and joyful – when we're in love; he's there to comfort us when things go wrong. In short, he's not just there to talk to when we're in a church or a prayer meeting, or when we need his specific help. He's always there, always on. We are satellites and he's Ground Control; he wants constant connection with us. And I promise you, if you open up a channel of communication with God, and keep it open – You. Will. Thrive.

4. WORSHIP

Christians love singing. We are really, weirdly keen on it. There's probably no place other than your local church where you'd find more people gathering together each week to belt out a tune, perhaps apart from a sports stadium or a pop concert. But even fans take breaks. Christians are *relentless.*

Normally, that ends with something halfway to beautiful. Sometimes, it results in something truly magnificent, like Handel's *Messiah* or The Jonas Brothers' *Sucker.* But sometimes, it can go really badly wrong . . .

A few years ago, I was at a breakfast meeting with a group of adult Christians. Once we'd eaten, the obvious next thing for us to do was sing – because, as I said, *Christians love singing* – and so a guy who had planned a little setlist got out his guitar and began to 'lead worship'. This is the part of any Christian gathering when we all face the same way and sing to God, led by an individual or a small band. Bizarrely, and quite by coincidence, he'd planned a list of songs that all had the same central idea: separate male and female parts. They all had a kind of call and response thing going on: men sing a line, women sing a line, then both groups sing together, and repeat.

If you're interested, I remember the first song was called 'For this purpose', by a singer–songwriter named Graham Kendrick,* and we should definitely bring it back. I like it because, unlike a lot of the other songs that Christians sing, which can sometimes be mostly about us, it's completely focused on Jesus. And it seems to me that if you're going to sing to Jesus, it would make sense that the song was actually about him. We'll talk more about that later.

**Graham Kendrick is like the Dr Dre of worship music. He wrote all the bangers; sadly for him, he didn't also invent an incredibly lucrative range of headphones.*

The second song was also like this, and then so was the third. A male singing part, followed by a female singing part. Which is not particularly a problem, except for one thing. This was an event for *men only.*

The obvious solution would have been to stop and sing a different song; one that didn't have whole sections intended for women. As a gathering of *British* men, however, we certainly didn't want to cause that kind of social embarrassment for the poor guy who'd picked the songs. So, as the realization dawned on us, we did the only thing we could do; some of us started pretending to be women. I distinctly remember putting on a high-pitched voice and belting out 'rise up women of the church' in a room that could barely contain its awkwardness. In that particular song, there was even an entire verse that was meant to be sung by female voices only. Reader, I did my very best.

In truth this wasn't an act of worship but of endurance, and we saw it through because, well, *singing is what you do* when you're a Christian. Music is tightly connected to almost every expression of following Jesus around the world and through history – from the psalms of King David to the chants of monks, through to gospel choirs and modern-day worship leaders who don't think through their song choices. There are lots of good reasons for this: music enables us to communicate emotionally; singing together can be an amazing expression of community, and the Bible actually suggests it's a good idea.* But, while you'd be forgiven for making this mistake, worship isn't about music.

**Psalm 150 tells you to praise God with the 'timbrel', which is a kind of tambourine, and because of this one line the church of the 1970s and 80s was a very weird place.*

I don't mean that worship music isn't worship, obviously. But especially in the Western Church of the last few years, we've begun to act as though singing is all that worship is. As if all that matters to God is that we congregate regularly and sing nice but repetitive ditties which, truthfully, would fit best in the 1980s' power ballad genre. I think God's desire for our worship is a lot bigger than that, and not because he needs his ego to be stroked. God wants us to worship him because truly doing so can completely transform us.

*

We all worship something. I'm yet to meet someone who doesn't. For some people it's a partner – someone to whom they are utterly devoted – for others it's their children, or even, in some cases that won't make sense if you're currently a teenager, their parents. The word itself is derived from 'worth-ship', literally meaning that we decide something is worthy of our devotion and adoration. Some people worship a sports team (there are grown adults who never cry, except when their club loses a cup final in the last minute), and others swear their love for singers, film stars and celebrities. Everybody has that one thing, above all else, that commands their unswerving loyalty and love.

I wish I could tell you a fabulous story from my past at this point. That I was obsessed with Ferrari cars and saved up for a trip to Italy to see them being test-raced. The truth, however, is that while I did worship something in my teens, there's no way to make it cool.

Because, you see, the object of *my* worship was the long-running BBC television sci-fi series *Doctor Who.*

I was totally, tragically obsessed with the show – and yes, long before it was even slightly cool. My room was a shrine, filled with toy daleks and posters of Tom Baker (the greatest of all Doctors). I had 180 books, and around 70 VHS video cassettes – each containing a super-low-definition recording of a low-budget TV show with wobbly sets and incomprehensibly cheap monster costumes. And if there was ever even the slightest chance that I might miss a new episode when it aired, I would feign sickness or lock myself in my room to avoid whatever important engagement was threatening my date with the Doctor.

I didn't just demonstrate my love for the show by obsessively re-watching and spending all my money on it, though. I also made pilgrimages to meet the stars; I once made my dad queue for five hours so that I could get one of my books signed by then-Doctor Sylvester McCoy.* I joined *Doctor Who* appreciation clubs, and subscribed to the official magazine. If there was a way to have more of *Doctor Who* in my life, I would have attempted it.

**My dad has never forgotten or forgiven me for this lost Saturday.*

Though I wasn't in the top league of *Doctor Who* fans who went to conventions and spent their evenings writing weird fan fiction, I did worship it. I decided that – as desperately sad and misspent as my youth now sounds – *Doctor Who* was worthy of being the object of my love, my money, my time and many of my decisions. It was so worthy that I was prepared to be mocked by my friends for admitting my passion. Because that's what you give to something you truly worship. Not only do you transmit great value towards that thing or person, but you also inevitably change as a result.*

**In my case, I became chubbier and less attractive to anyone who knew about my obsession.*

If you worship your children as a parent, you invest your love, your money (believe me) and your time, and almost every decision you make is influenced or defined by your desire to make them happy and safe. If you worship a husband, wife, boyfriend or girlfriend, the same is true. And when we do this, not only does the person on the receiving end get to experience being truly loved, but we change too. The things we do, and the way we choose to do them, are all changed and defined by this relationship with the top priority in our lives. And outside of ourselves, a watching world knows us and even categorizes us by what we worship. It is the chief way in which we become affiliated, and even known – devoted husband; loving father; West Ham United fan; *Doctor Who* tragic.

We were made to worship. It actually feels pretty natural to put something in pole position; something outside of ourselves that we've decided is 'worthy'. But the truth is that we weren't made to worship TV shows of questionable quality, or wives or husbands, or even children. Of course we should love and cherish them – and it's even okay to have a weird fascination with a TV show – but none of them are as worthy as the one thing, the one person, that we were literally *made* to worship.

*

God is worth our devotion. More than anything else in the world; more than anyone in the world. More than the people we love most; more than the things we value most highly.

Easy to say, isn't it? Much more difficult to put into practice. Because even if you agree that God *is* real and therefore not only the Creator of the whole universe, but also the rescuer of everything that is broken within it, he's still invisible. And because of that, it can be quite easy for us to forget about him when we're faced with far less impressive but far more obvious 'gods'. There is no way to argue that FC Barcelona or Taylor Swift or road cycling is more 'worthy' than God – but they're all much more immediate, much easier to grasp.

This is not a new thing. Way back in the first part of the Bible (the Old Testament), when God's people had to depend on him much more directly for survival, they were constantly forgetting him and putting other things in his place. That's why, when Moses – their then leader – went up a mountain to receive ten 'commandments' about how God wanted them to live, the very first one was 'You shall have no other Gods before me'. That was the first one on the list – the most important one of all. By comparison, 'You shall not murder' was sixth. The first thing God wanted to tell his people: don't worship other 'gods' ahead of me.

And of course, we immediately find out why. As soon as Moses descends from the mountain, where the people all know he's literally gone to speak directly with God, he finds that they couldn't even keep their religious devotion together for a few weeks. He's been away for 40 days – and by that time they've become so tired of waiting for him to return that they melt down all their gold and create a new 'god': a statue of a golden calf to worship instead.* They didn't take very long to lose their faith in the God in whom they'd previously placed their trust.

**You can find all this in Exodus 32. Moses, in the style of a Guy Ritchie film, kicks off big time like a nutter when he comes down the mountain and spots the big gold cow.*

These people had just witnessed incredible miracles – wondrous signs that God was real and with them. They had walked across the bed of the Red Sea, with walls of water held back on either side of them like a scene from a superhero film. They had survived ten miraculous plagues that had devastated the captors who had enslaved them in

Egypt. All of this and yet they were already so forgetful that they were starting to construct their own gods, built to look like a gigantic version of an ornament that your gran brought back from holiday. And the thing is, if we're honest, we do this too. We have so many reasons to remember God's greatness, yet we're constantly distracted by the idols in front of us, however silly and feeble they might be in comparison with him: sex, money, sport . . . even a TV show.

It's easy to say that God is worth our devotion, but the truth is that giving it to him requires a **choice** from us. We have to choose to give him everything; to put him at the centre of our lives, which is where he belongs. And that's what worship really is.

So how do we truly put God in pole position, above anything else? I think some of the answer is in how we spend our resources: our money, our time and our attention. But sitting above all of this is something far bigger. I think true worship is about surrender.

That probably sounds like quite a negative word. Surrender is what people do when they're being overwhelmed, usually by an attacking force, but that's not what I mean. I'm not suggesting that we have to wave some sort of imaginary white flag to God. But it does mean recognizing that there's a way in which we might choose to live that isn't good for us – where we live for ourselves, indulge to excess, accumulate as much as we can and forget to care who we hurt in the process – and another, better way to live. It means realizing that God deserves to be honoured not only by our words but also by our actions, our lifestyles, and deciding to choose his way of life above our own. Surrender is letting go of what we want, in order to embrace what he wants for us.

We were never meant to be number one in our lives; never meant to be the centre of our own worlds. That place is reserved for

God – who created us, our entire world and the eternity that we're welcomed into. And when we put him in that place, when we decide that he is *worthy*, it is natural for us to seek out what he wants for our lives, rather than what we might seek out by our own instinct. That's what it means, in a nutshell, to follow him. We declare his worth-ship through our lifestyle.

If that sounds a bit abstract and weird, the good news is that he kept it fairly straightforward for us. We don't have to guess what his way looks like; we don't even just have to follow an instruction manual and a list of rules.* God has given us a living, breathing example to follow – an incredible, ultimate role model to try to imitate: Jesus.

**The Bible really isn't just a list of rules to be enacted word for word – otherwise we'd all still be burying our own poo outside our houses (see Deuteronomy 23.13).*

One of the most fascinating things about the Bible is that the story of Jesus is told four times, from four different perspectives. Have you ever stopped to consider how unbelievably groundbreaking that is? If someone made a film that did that today they'd be considered an artistic genius. Because of these four books – Matthew, Mark, Luke and John – we get to see loads of different insights from Jesus' life. We get to read what he said about stuff like money, relationships and how to treat people; we watch how he interacted with others and how he spent and prioritized his time – basically, we get to see exactly how he lived. Reading, picturing, talking about and understanding how Jesus lived gives us a kind of blueprint for our own lifestyle choices.

Have you ever tried to learn a dance routine? The kids in my life sometimes amuse themselves by trying to teach me one, and without exception it always ends in personal humiliation, and occasionally a semi-serious back injury. But if you have tried to learn a dance, you'll know that the best way to do so is by imitating someone who already knows the moves. That is much, much easier than the alternative: reading or being told a series of steps as cold, descriptive statements like 'right foot forward, pivot, left arm swivel . . .'. In so many areas of life, we learn best by watching someone else go first.

In the Bible, Jesus is literally followed around by a group of people (specifically those 12 we mentioned), who learn to be like him by watching his every move. That was how it worked in their culture: people would find a 'rabbi' (religious leader) to follow, and they'd literally imitate him.* We obviously can't do that in the same way because Jesus isn't walking around as a living, breathing man any more, and so we have to take our cues from what we read about him in the Bible.

**I wonder if some of them tried to do his voice?!*

Paul, writing a little later in the New Testament, says that we should 'follow God's example' (Ephesians 5.1), although that can also be translated as 'be imitators of Christ'. To demonstrate, this is what following Jesus might look like in a few contentious areas of everyday life, based on what we see and hear of him in the Bible:

- ***Money.*** I met a guy once who tried to convince me that Jesus was a successful businessman with a number of houses, a string of employees and significant personal wealth. This view may have been *slightly* influenced by the fact that this man was himself a wealthy and successful businessman, but sadly it's absolute nonsense. Jesus was so uninterested in personal accumulation that he spent his time relying on the hospitality of others in order to have a bed for the night. He convinced business people to throw away everything and follow him instead, and he told the rich ruler whom he famously met that 'it is easier for a camel to pass through the eye of a needle than for someone who is rich to enter the kingdom of God' (Matthew 19.24). Jesus talked about money *a lot* – and the overall message was not to hoard it but to be generous. This is a massive challenge, isn't it? Because, let's be honest, having money is much nicer than not having it. But I think Jesus knew just how easy it was to become overwhelmed by wealth, so he warned us to be careful of it.

- ***Relationships and sex.*** Jesus doesn't talk a lot (all right, at all) about boyfriends and girlfriends, so we have to look at his life for some clues about what it would mean to follow him in the way we conduct our relationships.* What we *do* know is that he treated everyone with the utmost respect and humanity, that he never objectified anyone, and that he talked constantly about putting other people first. These are fantastic ground rules for any relationship, including those we might have with a romantic partner, and they also have something to say to our sex-mad, objectifying culture. I'm absolutely certain that the Jesus we see in the Bible, treating women as equals, would hate the very idea of pornography. It's also worth saying that he seemed to have a pretty wild time as a single man without needing any sort of sexual gratification. It's possible he'd think our culture was a little bit obsessed with the constant desire for sex and romance.
  **Just in case anyone is scouring this book for religious heresy, I'm not suggesting Jesus might have had a girlfriend, or indeed a boyfriend.*

- ***Politics.*** Well, this is a tricky one. People from every end of the political spectrum, throughout history, have tried to claim Jesus was on their side – and yes, that includes the Nazis. Plenty of other people prefer to go the other way and claim that Jesus wasn't political at all. The truth, however, is more complicated: he was *very* political, but you can't really neatly stick any sort of political badge on him. Looking at the evidence we have in the Bible, we see that Jesus absolutely was political – he made comments on paying tax and how the poor should be treated, for example – but it's far too simplistic to suggest that he aligns with any political *party*. Following Jesus definitely does mean engaging with politics, though, and caring about what happens in our society; you can't ignore the world's problems because you want to focus on being a Christian. It's part of the deal.

- ***Alcohol and parties.*** It may surprise you that Jesus was no party-pooper. In fact, his first miracle (the wedding in John 2) involved replenishing the stocks of wine when they'd run out. Does that mean Jesus was in favour of getting completely drunk? I don't think so – he trusted people to decide for themselves when it was time to switch to lemonade – but it does suggest that he was totally fine with people enjoying themselves. In fact, Jesus was always out at one dinner party or another. For him, the whole point of going out for food and drink was to spend time with his friends, not to see what funny stories he could generate by persuading them to do another tequila. When we get invited to parties, the culture around them suggests that drinking crazy amounts of alcohol – and even experimenting with illegal drugs – will be the key to having a great time. It's not true – in fact, that is usually the way to mistakes, regret and some unpleasant physical side-effects. Following the example of Jesus means enjoying ourselves, but remembering that the best way to do that is to spend time with the people we care about.

God cares about these and every other area of our lives. And here's the point: you don't have to make positive, God-honouring decisions about your lifestyle because God is sitting there with a big book of rules, just waiting for you to step out of line. As Christians, we make those choices because it's a way of signalling to God that he's number one in our lives. But the reason God has views on how we live our lives is that he actually knows what's best for us. So – as we follow Jesus, and show God that we love him, we in turn change for the better. That's why the Bible talks a lot about 'being transformed' as we follow Jesus; becoming more like him makes us better people too.*

**I'm terrible at learning Bible verses, and always have been. But one of my absolute favourites is, 'Do not conform to the pattern of this world, but be transformed by the renewing of your mind.' This little verse – Romans 12.2 – manages to express in 18 words what I've barely been able to communicate in several thousand: choosing God's way above ours transforms us for the better.*

This is the heart of what it means to worship God; to demonstrate to him that he is worth everything. Our lives become defined by our first love, and people who know us begin to see us through the lens of that passion. LA Lakers fan, MCU nut . . . Christian.

*

So, finally, let's go back to that indescribably awkward Bible study breakfast, the one with the male and female song parts and a room full of men. Why did we need to sing at all? Why couldn't we just have honoured God and demonstrated his worth in the way that we talked and ate bacon? Well, to some extent, we could have done that, but, as I said before, Christians *love* singing. And there's a good reason for that: when we know God, and we understand who he is and what he's done for us, we have a natural instinct not just to namecheck and follow God but to actively worship him. As in perform an *act* of worship.

This can take many forms – like reading out specially written words called liturgies alone or together, or like dancing, or performing music or poetry. But perhaps the most simple and obvious act of worship for our culture is to sing; after all, it's what we already do to express our devotion to sports teams, our favourite bands, and even, in some weird cases, a politician. And so we sing together – in our churches, our festivals and events, and in smaller groups like that funny little Bible study. Perhaps just as significantly, we can sing on our own – in the shower or on a walk in the woods, or when we're home alone. In both cases we do it because, when we start to know God better, we almost can't help it. Worshipping God is something of an instinct.

There's a famous sermon, preached by an American Baptist minister called S. M. Lockridge,* which has been called the greatest of all time. It's become affectionately known by one of its repeating phrases – 'that's my King' – and while it was *technically* a sermon, really the delivery of the preacher turns it into a piece of performance poetry. There are countless recordings of it online – I heartily recommend you look it up and listen immediately.

**That stood for Shadrach Meshach Lockridge, which is one of the coolest names ever but also feels as if it's missing something. That's one for the Bible geeks (see Daniel 3).*

'That's my King' is a fast-moving, breathless attempt to talk about and explain who Jesus is. It feels as fresh and striking today as it did when it was first preached and recorded in the 1950s. In line after line, Lockridge pulls out yet another true fact about Jesus that makes him 'worthy' of our devotion and praise. Every single item is another reminder of just how magnificent our God is. Here's just part of it:

> Do you know Him?
> He's the greatest phenomenon that ever crossed the horizon of this world. He's God's Son.
> He's a sinner's Saviour.
> He's the centre-piece of civilization.
> He stands in the solitude of Himself.

He's awesome.
He's unique.
He's unparalleled.
He's unprecedented.
He's the loftiest idea in literature.
He's the highest personality in philosophy.
He's the supreme problem in higher criticism.
He's the fundamental doctrine of true theology.
He's the cardinal necessity of spiritual religion.
He's the miracle of the age.
He's the superlative of everything good that you choose to call Him.
He's the only one qualified to be an all-sufficient Saviour
I wonder if you know Him today?
(From a sermon by S. M. Lockridge (1913–2000), preached while he was Pastor of Calvary Baptist Church, San Diego, where he was on the staff from 1953 to 1993)

If you do know him, then as you read this perhaps you feel that swell of inspiration to worship him. Not just with song but by the way in which you choose to live your life; stepping towards him with every decision you make, instead of stepping away. Because, if he really is 'the centre-piece of civilization', then he's worth everything, *everything* we have.

5.

FAMILY

Imagine you're walking into a church. Not your ideal version of what a church should be but an *average* church. What does it feel like as you walk through those doors? Is it a positive feeling? Is it a place where you naturally think you'll be *welcome*? Where people will talk to you, and probably even be nice to you? Is it warm, comfortable and overwhelmingly kind? Is it a place where you think God – if he was anywhere – might spend some of his time?

Or is it a different feeling – more negative? Is it a place where you're slightly scared to walk through the door? Where you've got a feeling that people will judge you; won't like you; won't have anything in common with you? Do you imagine it as cold and uninviting – the sort of place you'd never voluntarily spend any time and that you'd only ever enter under the duress of a school trip?

Every one of us has a slightly different expectation when we imagine the average church, and that has a lot to do with our experience of churches, and of the people who tend to fill them. There are some brilliant churches, and then there are some that, to be kind, might have forgotten to be quite so welcoming, somewhere along the way. Some of them, sadly, have even become better known for everything they stand against than anything they stand *for*. If you've experienced one of those churches, then you might be forgiven for not feeling all that positive about them.

And yet, despite all the mistakes that churches make – not all of which should be easily forgiven – going to church is part of being a follower of Jesus. Not because God really likes the buildings, the religious language and all the old people, but because of something much more important. We join *a* church because all those local churches – the ones we might join and the ones we'd probably never think of walking into – are part of a massive, global movement, which is confusingly also called *the* Church.

To put it simply: a church is a local gathering of Christians. It's not the building, it's the group of people. If those people relocate to a sports hall, or to a new building, then that church has moved. Or, to put it another way, if some sort of alien death ray vaporized the building but left the people still standing there, then the church would have survived. But then that local congregation is only one of the estimated 37 million churches all around the world, all of which sprang up out of a single source: the early church that we read about in the Bible, in the book of Acts (more in a minute on this).

Now, even though that single root has splintered out into the 37 million local ones, every single one of them is united together as part of *the* Church.* All of the individual churches together form the Church, just as a local gang of meerkats is still part of the world's total meerkat family (terrible example). Jesus talks about this in Matthew 16, when he says he's going to build his church. He's not suggesting that he's going to build a building; he's saying that across time and all over the world, he's going to develop his family in millions of places at once. It's all one thing. It's a gigantic, worldwide family, and when we choose to follow Jesus, we become part of that family, like it or not.

**All right, not every single one. Some of them have lost their way a bit and started adding weird bits to the stuff Jesus taught. But the vast majority are part of the family.*

You know how they say that you can choose your friends, but you can't choose your family? That's kind of how it works with *the* Church. There are lots of weird, wonderful and frankly not-so-wonderful gatherings of people all around the planet – a surfers' church on the coast of Cornwall; congregations that conduct their entire service in Latin and swing balls of burning incense around as they do; churches held in sports stadiums; secret underground groups in places where Christianity is banned . . . and, yes, that one round the corner from you that you've never set foot in. All of them are joined together by the same thing, the same incredible person: we are, all together, the family of Jesus.

Of course, the word 'family' might not have the best associations for you. I pray that you've experienced a wonderful family, with loving parents and perhaps siblings or other relatives who bring light to your life. But I'm aware that for some of us that just isn't how it is or was. Sometimes families let us down badly, hurt us, abandon us and even abuse us. Families are messy and, in some cases, broken. If that's been your experience, I'm sorry. It's not fair.

I wish I could say at this point that the family of God will never let you down like that, but, honestly, that's not a promise that anyone can make. While it belongs to God, this family is completely made up of people – broken, fallible people like you and me. We do let each other down, and sometimes that happens in the supposedly safe places of churches. I believe that the fact that some Christians have used church as a vehicle for pain and abuse makes God really mad. It should make us mad too – but there's no point denying that it happens. Again, if that's happened to you: that's not right, and I'm sorry.

What we can do, however, is decide that the Church isn't going to continue to be like that any longer. Because we – and really I mean *you* now – are the emerging generations of this church family. We are taking our place to lead and shape the Church of the future, and we can decide that some of the horrors, scandals and abuses of power of the past will not be repeated. We can decide that all the great bits of the Church are the things that remain in the future. And our best chance of doing that is by learning again what it really means to be the family of God. Because while it's important to acknowledge our weaknesses and failures, the Church is quite an amazing thing – an unparalleled source of kindness and good in our world, and often the place where we can experience the love of God most clearly. Perhaps we just need to look back at how it started . . .

*

In chapter two of the book of Acts, Jesus has just left the earth, and in his place the Holy Spirit has arrived.* His followers – shell-shocked by a series of dramatic events – are for the moment sticking together in one place, living together as a small community. The last few verses of that chapter describe a tightly bonded group: people living alongside and caring for each other and putting each other first.

**This makes it sound a bit like a substitution in a football match. And actually that's not the worst analogy in the world. We'll look at this in much more detail in the next chapter.*

This is probably the earliest record that we have of a 'church', and it sounds like a pretty good one. They worship God together, and they see miraculous things happening in their midst on a daily basis – the sort of stuff that 'fills people with awe'. They are also communists, which doesn't mean that they're Russian spies from the 1960s but that they hold everything in common. What's yours is mine, and vice versa.

If someone is in need, members of the church sell their possessions or even their property to raise money to sort it out. They meet together every single day, and they have this constant kind of joy that they all carry around with them. And guess what? That church grows in size, day after day, as more and more people catch sight of what they have and realize it's better than anything else in the world.

If we're honest, there aren't many churches today that look very much like that early incarnation, which is kind of weird considering it's the blueprint that the Bible gives us for church. You can see how it happened, though; we like having our own stuff and our own space, meeting every day is quite inconvenient, and communism definitely has a bad rep. But I think that if we could get our act together, this is what church *should* be like. Everyone cared for, everyone close – like a really great family.

Let me repeat myself: just because church hasn't looked very much like this over the course of the last century in particular, doesn't mean it can't do so again. Just because other generations of Christians have looked at that blueprint and decided to create churches that include inequality, exclusion and even abuse, doesn't mean that the rising generations have to do the same. We've still got access to the original plans.

*

If you had to choose one word to sum up our culture, I wonder what it would be. 'Distracted', maybe, given how much time we all spend staring at constantly pinging devices? Or how about 'consumeristic', which describes not only our obsession with hording material *stuff*, but also the way we view so much of our lives – including friendships and relationships – as transactions? There are probably a few good answers, but I would choose the word 'individualistic'. I think that we're not only pretty self-obsessed as a culture but we've lost our broad sense of connection with one another. We're not so much a unified human race as 8 billion individuals.

If you want to understand what a culture values, then look at what it dreams about. You might be familiar with the idea of 'the American Dream' – the thought that every individual could own their own home, drive a great car, marry their perfect mate and raise beautiful children. That aspiration isn't just confined to America – it's been exported and caught globally – particularly in the West but increasingly all over the world. This idea, popularized in the 1950s, was pretty individualistic to start with, but in the decades that have followed, it has become even less about community and family. To begin with, the American Dream was also about creating flourishing towns full of perfect little families, all over a prospering United States. Now even those ideas have shrunk; people jump between jobs in an effort to scale the career ladder as quickly as possible, and move around their country and even the globe as if they're playing a board game. And that semi-selfless idea of creating a great family that allows us to think beyond ourselves? Well, now those families are only part of the dream until they're not working any more – at which point we fracture them off in pursuit of something that better suits our individual needs.

Meanwhile, as the privileged few of us are able to pursue all our constant personal goals, vast sections of the global population suffer. Because of the pursuit of individual wealth, a relative minority of people get to live some version of the American Dream (now alive and well in every continent), while the majority of individuals suffer. Because we've created a world where there's no limit on what one person can own, or how much power they can wield, there are now individual men who have more money than entire countries.*

**There are incredibly selfish women-who'll-stop-at-nothing too; they've just got a bit of catching up to do in the male-dominated world of mega-wealth.*

Sounds a little bit broken, doesn't it? It isn't meant to be like this. And I think those few short verses in Acts 2 give us a pretty strong hint at what a better alternative might look like. I'm not suggesting we all need to sell everything we have and live together in communes, but I do think that seeing our connectedness to others is vitally important. Individualism tries to prise us apart from each other; God has always wanted us to think of ourselves as a community of fellow humans.

If you walk into a church today, or listen to a modern Christian worship song, or even pick up a Christian book, there's a good chance you could miss this point. Because as the world around us has got ever more focused on 'me',* the Church seems to have accidentally fallen into the same trap and made the Bible into the story of how the God who made the universe is seeking to rebuild his broken relationship with billions of individuals, and then set them off on billions of individual missions around his world.

**No, not actually me. I can barely even get my dog to listen to me. I mean 'us', the individual.*

Now, in a way, that *is* actually true. God does have the power and the desire to know each one of us personally, and he does seem to have specific plans for individuals. He uses certain people at certain times to accomplish parts of his greater plan for the world. But that is not the main thing; it's not the entire point of it all.

From the very beginning of the Bible, God is in a relationship with a group of people. In the first story, it's just two people – a young couple starting out, with only a garden and a really shifty-looking pet snake to their names. But after them, God begins a relationship with a family, which then grows up into an entire nation: Israel. Yes, his friendship with specific individuals within that nation is important, but when God gives out commandments and promises, he's giving them out to the whole community. When he tells Moses, 'You shall have no other gods before me' (Exodus 20.2), he's not only talking to Moses – he's talking to their entire culture.

All through the ancient history documented in the Old Testament, people understood that they were part of a community; a family headed up by God himself. Like a sort of nice version of the mafia. They were a people and, while their individual actions mattered, what mattered even more was how all those actions added up to the behaviour of the community. So it mattered that you treated your servant well, but it mattered even more that the whole people believed in and acted out justice. Every single individual playing their part in creating a culture of living God's way.

This was still the case when Jesus arrived. Of course he related to individuals, but he was also always talking to *a people*. At first when we read the story, it seems as if he's still just talking to Israel, but as he goes on we start to realize that he's opening up his message of love and salvation to everyone. In Matthew 24.14, he says that before the world as we know it ends, 'this gospel of the kingdom will be preached in the whole world as a testimony to *all nations*'. After his death and resurrection, that's exactly what the early Church busied themselves with doing. But here's the important distinction: they weren't just aiming to convert individuals everywhere – they wanted to show *entire countries* the way to God. And in some parts of the world, including the one in which I'm currently writing, that's exactly what happened.

God is interested in the details of our lives – our hopes and dreams. He is a perfect, loving Father, and as such he knows each of his kids in obsessive detail. By comparison, I am an utterly terrible father, and yet I still spend my life fascinated by the different individual lives that my four children are building. I'm massively invested in my daughter Naomi's sporting activities; I love listening to my youngest son Zachary talk in detail about his day; I could build Lego with my middle son Samuel for ever; and I enjoy nothing more than trading *Brooklyn Nine-Nine* quotes with my eldest, Joel. God has exactly the same sort of list of joys when it comes to his children – it's just that the list is several billion names long.

The thing is, while my wife and I love our children as individuals, we also love them as a family, and we have hopes and dreams for the sort of family we might be. We want our family to act collectively as a force of good in the world, to be a group of people who so radiate love for one another and the world around us that it ends up influencing a whole host of other people around us. In fact, our hope for our family is that it might even make an impression on – have an influence on – our entire community.

God has always had plans for humanity that work on the smallest and the biggest possible level, and every stage in between. In some crazy, hard-to-fathom way, God feels our pain when we slip over as children and graze our knees,* and also cares about the large-scale activities of the entire human race – war, peace, our role in climate change, and more.

**In Psalm 139, it actually says that he knew us even when we were tiny foetuses being formed in the womb. Get your head around that.*

The thing is, we turned our backs on God and his plan for us. We did that as historic individuals, and we still do it today; every time someone understands who God is and yet decides not to follow him, that act of stepping away from him is repeated again. But it's not just people who've done that, *peoples* have done that too. Entire nations, or at least the vast majority within them, have said 'no thanks' to God. We read about a few of those places in the Bible, and we know many of them today; perhaps we even live in one.

This act of turning our backs and living for ourselves instead of the way we were made to be is essentially what sin is. 'Sin' is an old-fashioned, unfashionable word, mainly because it means admitting that we're not allowed to do whatever we like. But again, individualism has caused us to fixate on sin as a personal issue, when it's actually much bigger than that. Sure, when you punch your kid sister in the arm, that is a mark of you stepping away from God's best way of living. But that's not all sin is; it's not just about the small (and sometimes big) ways in which we mess up. It's also about much bigger stuff – the systems in our world that are broken. Sin is also about how entire cultures turn their backs on God's way.

Racism is sin. Not just the individual act which sees one person tear another down with an insult because of the colour of their skin, but the broken system that means one person was always going to get an easier journey through school and then university, and then a top job, because their skin colour was different from someone else's. Sexism is sin – not just in terms of individual circumstances, but in the landscape behind those circumstances that allowed them to happen in the first place. The #metoo movement is the story of many awful sins, but it's also about a wider system of sin. Same goes for poverty, climate injustice, sexual abuse, drugs . . . and I could go on.

Now, what happens when you read this famous verse, written by Paul in the New Testament, through the filter of that understanding of sin?

> God demonstrates his own love for us in this: while we were still sinners, Christ died for us.
> (Romans 5.8)

God sent his only Son to die, in order to break the power of sin. And yes, Jesus died for us – individuals who do unkind things to ourselves and each other – but he also died for *us*, the peoples and nations and cultures of the world. He died in order to break the power of every evil we see in our world today. Not only that: he also came to establish a better way of living. And he chooses to do that through us – his gathered family.

The Christian faith isn't about you, or me, or my friend Brenda being reconciled to God.* It's about a whole family – as big as possible – joining his revolution to remake the world as it was supposed to be. We have to own our part in that, which we call repentance, and we have to ask God's forgiveness that we didn't wake up sooner. But then, with God's power behind us and his love in our hearts, we join together with our newfound brothers and sisters to make the world a better place. That's the whole point of the Church.

**I don't know anyone called Brenda. This was a figure of speech. Sorry, Brendas.*

*

This all feels like a pretty sweet deal, right? Instinctively, when we lower our defences and think about it, when we understand that the all-powerful being behind the universe is actually a loving Father who wants to invite us to be a part of his family, it's hard to find a good reason to say no. More than that, it's the sort of offer we'd probably want to pass on to as many other people as we possibly could.

In a world with so much pain, so much injustice and inequality, so much fear – this news is great for *everyone*. All of us – any of us, from the richest to the poorest – get to be offered a seat at the Father's table. And that's why, throughout history, the Church has been famous for throwing wide its doors to anyone and everyone, no matter what their background, behaviour, gender, race, age or sexuality. It doesn't matter who you are, we say: come and join the family!

In the unlikely event that you haven't spotted my sarcasm here, I'd better underline it. The Church, throughout history and even today, is not exactly known for this kind of arms-open-wide acceptance. At some points in the past, certain wings of the Church executed people for not believing exactly the right things, and even if we don't do that any more, parts of this family are still far better known for keeping people out than welcoming them in. There are lots of quite complicated reasons for this,* but in essence they all boil down to the same thing: we can't get our heads around the enormity of God's love. We can't understand how he can find *us* loveable, let alone people who we think have fallen even further from God's way than we have.

**Some people are going to read this and feel extremely grumpy. They may even think that I'm not a good fit for the family. But for them: I've simplified a lot of very important issues here. Churches are allowed to have different views on what the Bible says about different things as long as we don't start changing what's actually written in it and we see people as God does: children to be loved, not problems to be solved.*

John writes: 'let us love one another, for love comes from God. Everyone who loves has been born of God and knows God. Whoever does not love does not know God, because God is love' (1 John 4.7–8). And Jesus says, '*Whoever* believes in the Son has eternal life' (John 3.36). So God is love and, because of his great love for us all, whoever believes in his Son is invited to the everlasting family BBQ that is heaven. There are no exceptions, no clauses. God loves you. It's as straightforward as that.

Maybe you've been led to believe that there's something about you that makes you unloveable or even unacceptable to God. Something you've done or maybe even something you *are*. Or perhaps there are people around you who feel that way. So just to be crystal clear: if you're black or white, gay or straight, rich or poor, trans or cis, able-bodied or disabled – God loves you and he wants you in his family. If you can't hold anything together; if you've done something awful; if you can't stand yourself – God loves you and he wants you in his family. If your mental health keeps diving; if you can't stop hurting the people around you; if you are just so 'normal' that you feel you're probably not doing life right – God loves you, with an everlasting love,* and he wants to give you a seat at his table.

**This phrase is found in Jeremiah 31.3 and expresses the level of love that God has for his people; God loves us for ever and ever and ever.*

In the long term, that table is eternal and heavenly. But right now, the table is meant to exist in the Church; in the millions of local family gatherings all around the world. We are meant to extend that invitation – that offer to come and be part of God's family – to absolutely everyone, no exceptions.

When I was a teenager, growing up in a Christian youth group, I imagined this kind of open-heartedness came naturally. But that was until the youth leaders decided to try to integrate into our youth group a lad who had both a learning disability and a serious sight issue. There were some aspects to this guy's behaviour that (though quite understandable) were slightly frustrating to me as a teenager. And although I'm ashamed of it now, I found this lad – let's call him Paul – *annoying.* He messed up games and was loud; he shouted out random stuff during the supposedly quiet parts of our youth group sessions. Of course he did; he saw the world very differently from us, and the things we found easy were difficult for him. Every day for Paul's family was complicated and sometimes painful, and the fact that a local youth group was welcoming him in probably brought immense relief to his parents and, while he didn't show it, was helping him to feel as though he belonged somewhere too.

But at the time, I didn't really care about any of that. All I cared about was the fact that Paul was messing up my safe space, *my* place to belong. So I was horrible to him. I left him out of things; I made zero effort to become his friend. When leaders asked me to include him, I found a way not to. In the end, Paul got too old for the group and wasn't allowed to come any more. But as I think back on that time, I can't imagine that the few months he spent as part of our family made him feel he was ever really welcome.

This is not the way it's meant to be. I messed this up badly and I still feel sorry about it. God's family is not an exclusive group – there isn't meant to be a wall on any side, keeping out the people who don't behave quite like us; keeping out those who don't look like us. God's family is for everyone, and part of being a member is making sure that no one ever feels they're not welcome, that they don't belong.

*

When we come together as God's family, it can be a beautiful thing. In a world of empty individualism, church is a place where we can be part of something bigger and better than ourselves. It's a place where we can celebrate the amazing news that God is real and wants to know us, where we can recognize God's 'worth-ship' through songs and prayers and a thousand other creative acts. It's where we can ask for help and where we can offer help to others. It's somewhere we belong enough to feel safe, and feel safe enough to be honest that we haven't got it all together. It's a place where we learn how to grow up together into the people that we were always made to become.

This Church, this family, is thousands of years old and billions of members strong. It's the source of so much good in the world; so much kindness and hope. Where people are otherwise forgotten, it is so often the Church that steps in to fill the void. Like any family, it's far from perfect, but – also like any family – it has the potential to accomplish great things. And while it might sound like a line from a slightly cheesy song, it always only does this when it remembers to love.

Jesus said a lot of profound and important things, but when it comes to being his family, there's one command that stands above all others: 'By this everyone will know that you are my disciples, if you love one another' (John 13.35).

What sent people streaming to join the earliest church, day after day? The way they loved and cared for each other. Why do people find a place of belonging in a church today? Because they sense the same thing. As we build the Church of the future, this can never fall from the very centre of our view. In our family, it's all about how we love each other.

6. POWER

I think we're now safely past the point where you're allowed to plot-spoil *Avengers: Infinity War*, right?* The first half of the superhero epic that captivated comic book nerds the world over might just be a film that I'll never grow tired of talking about, and not just because of *that* ending.

**If you are still in that group of people who scream and cover their ears at this point, seriously, what have you been doing with your life?*

Just in case you've never been interested enough to watch – or if like me have the memory of a goldfish – I'll recap. Thanos, the fearsome purple-tinted warrior from the planet Titan, is travelling around the universe, gathering up the immensely powerful Infinity Stones: six coloured gems which each contain the power to control a different element of the universe. They're always heavily guarded by superheroes or protected by other complications, but somehow Thanos just manages to scoop them up one by one as if he's collecting stamps. Once he has the green one, he can manipulate time; the blue one allows him to create portals to travel instantly through space, and so on. Each one on its own is so powerful that with it the bearer can win entire battles or save a whole planet. Bring all six stones together, however, and you have access to an entirely different level of power.

That's what Thanos does as he assembles his ultimate weapon: the Infinity Gauntlet – a gigantic metal glove* that houses all six of the gems and grants the wearer all of his or her abilities. When wearing the fully completed Gauntlet, Thanos is able to control time, space, reality and more. Essentially, he becomes all-powerful; God-like.

**It's weird how uncool this sounds when you write it down, isn't it?*

Of course, he's not quite on a par with God (using the weapon just once almost kills him). But he only needs one shot, using it to enact his maniacal plan to wipe out half of the population of the universe. Thus *Avengers: Infinity War* ends on the darkest note imaginable, as people across the world simply disappear into the air; ash in the wind. Thankfully there's a sequel, but anyone who saw the film for the first time in a cinema will remember the aching sense of horror and hopelessness we all felt at this unhappy ending.

Thanos needed the stones in order to carry out his dark dream of 'rebalancing' the universe. But here's a somewhat-interesting question in the light of that world-shattering climax: what would you do if someone gave you all the power of the six infinity stones?

Maybe you'd think about curing global poverty, or bringing about lasting world peace? Or, if you're honest, turning yourself into a billionaire or a global fashion icon, or making yourself president of the world. It's hard to take this question seriously, of course, because the power contained in the infinity stones isn't real. No one could really have access to that much power, not in the real world . . .

But what if they could? What if you really did have access to ultimate power, which could overcome and change the rules of the universe? And what if that power didn't burn you half to death if you ever chose to use it, but could be used again and again? Think of what you could achieve; think of the good that you could do.

In fact, being able to engage with this kind of power is one of the core claims of the Christian faith. We don't just get to *observe* the awesome power of God, we also somehow get to *participate* in it. The Bible records countless stories of God's divine power making, saving, redeeming and redefining things on an epic scale, and in every case human beings are involved.* He wins battles from impossible positions; he allows the rules of physics, biology and even nature to be altered; he even turns around the widely accepted one-way journey of death. His power is absolute; sometimes he uses it to intervene in the normal course of the world, and when he does, he chooses to use us as part of the action.

**Even including the creation of the world, although to be fair all he really lets the humans do in that story is name the animals.*

In fact, it's even more exciting than that. It's not just that when God decides he wants to do something different, weird or spectacular he grabs the nearest human and does it through them. No – God chooses to release some of his power to his people. Of all the human characters in the Bible who demonstrate miraculous, logic-defying powers, Jesus is by far the most prolific. And yet after he's performed a series of feats that would these days get him a 100-night residency in Las Vegas – water into wine, walking on water, feeding 5,000 and more – he says this:

> 'Very truly I tell you, whoever believes in me will do the works I have been doing, and they will do even greater things than these, because I am going to the Father. And I will do whatever you ask in my name, so that the Father may be glorified in the Son. You may ask me for anything in my name, and I will do it.' (John 14.12–14)

Did you catch that? 'Whoever believes in me will do the works I have been doing' – that's the kinds of miracles listed above – *and* 'they will do even greater things'. So, from Jesus' own mouth, we hear that God will give his people the power to do the miraculous. Things every bit as reality-bending as he did . . . and perhaps even more.

Now, I'm sure you're wondering at this point why – if this is to be taken seriously – we don't see a lot more miracles. How come our lakes and swimming pools aren't constantly full of hovering Christians? Why don't modern Jesus-followers save money on a Friday night by just buying a bottle of water and then turning it into a fabulous 1989 Bordeaux? But if we look beyond the very literal interpretation of this promise, we arguably do see the same power that Jesus called upon in the New Testament at work in the world today.

The sick are still healed today in Jesus' name. Not always – because God isn't Santa, and he doesn't just work through our list of requests and instantly tick them off – but sometimes. A few days ago, the youth group that I help to lead decided to pray, all at the same hour of the same day, for a 17-year-old lad who had been sick for weeks with an unidentified illness. He'd been in and out of hospital, to the point that his parents were becoming very worried. We prayed – calling on that same power that Jesus himself used – and from that very moment the boy began to quickly recover. It's perhaps a tiny example, but it seems to me that God is very happy to allow his power to work in tiny-seeming circumstances.

He's also prepared to use it on a larger scale too. When William Wilberforce helped to bring about the end of slavery in Britain and its empire, he called on the power of God to help him. During the famous Dunkirk evacuation in the Second World War – where Winston Churchill hoped to rescue 30,000 soldiers from slaughter in France – King George VI called a National Day of Prayer, and over ten times that number returned alive.* Those prayers unleashed a power so great that it changed the world. In their own way, both are arguably examples of Jesus' followers doing even 'greater things' in his name.

**I loved the film* Dunkirk. *I actually love everything Christopher Nolan does (if he made a film of a freshly painted wall, drying in real time, I would watch it) but I do wish he'd recognized the role that prayer may have had in averting disaster here.*

I'm mixing up my Disney franchises here, but perhaps the best popular-culture comparison for the power of God is the Force: the mythical energy source accessed by the Jedi in the *Star Wars* films. God's power is something that exists outside of us, flows through the fabric of the universe, and can be somehow harnessed by those who reach out to it. But unlike the Force, God's power can't be subverted for evil purposes, it isn't a shapeless, undefinable thing. God's power operates as a person with a name: the Holy Spirit.

The idea of the Holy Trinity – the Father, the Son (Jesus) and the Holy Spirit – is one of the hardest things for human beings to get their heads around. In one sense, I wonder if we're even meant to, or if the mind-bending strangeness of the idea is meant to be a clue that there are some mysteries that are just too big and clever to make sense of in this limited reality. Theologians, professors and other brainboxes have been trying to get on top of this idea for thousands of years, and still no one really has a perfect way to illustrate it. So with that in mind, let me leave it at this: all three are different and have equal status and yet all three are God. Each of the three plays a different role in the Bible, in history and in our lives today – although all three are present throughout.*

**Is this starting to get a bit heavy? Stick with me.*

Where the Old Testament is really focused on the Father, and the New Testament is where the Son takes centre stage, the Spirit is present through all of these parts of the Bible – from hovering over the water in Genesis 1 right through to empowering Jesus' miracles in the gospel stories. But after Jesus leaves the earth a short while after his resurrection, we see the Holy Spirit enter the world in a different and more visible way.

Just as Jesus had promised while he was still with his disciples, his departure marks the arrival of the Spirit. Think of it like a 'tag' between a team of two wrestlers in WWE (or don't, because WWE is ridiculous), or maybe as a baton passed between two relay runners. The disciples gather together, suddenly feeling very vulnerable and afraid after seeing their leader disappear into the clouds, and something crazy happens:

> Suddenly a sound like the blowing of a violent wind came from heaven and filled the whole house where they were sitting. They saw what seemed to be tongues of fire that separated and came to rest on each of them.
> (Acts 2.2–3)

I don't know how you imagine 'tongues of fire' when you try to picture them, because, to be honest, we don't see a lot of tongues made of anything apart from, well, tongue. In any case, what's really important is that through this moment, God released his power into the world – and into his Church – in a new way.

After that happens, the disciples (who become the early Church) start to experience and use God's power much more. Not only do they see supernatural things happening before their eyes, but they also witness the super-fast, sprawling growth of the Church. As discussed before, this wasn't just unlikely, it was completely against the odds. By all accounts, the cult of Jesus should have been shut down in a few months by killing off the disciples and threatening death to any new recruits. Yet despite the constant threat of death, the Church grew and spread like a supervirus. This could only possibly have happened because the power of God was flowing through the Church.

There was no point in history after that when God's power stopped moving, or when the Holy Spirit relaxed all this intensity. Which means: the same power that propelled the Church forward then is still around and available to us today. That's a big part of who the Holy Spirit is: the power of God, available and accessible to us. The Holy Spirit who heals the sick; the Holy Spirit who appears in crazy supernatural ways; the Holy Spirit who powers God's revolution in the world. He's the Infinity Gauntlet, in our hands.*

**Yes, I know, I've got a bit excited.*

We don't get to decide what God will do in a situation, because, well, he's God and he shouldn't be taking orders from someone like me, who once went out wearing two shoes from completely different pairs. What we can do is create space for God to move and then see what he does. We can have faith that something spectacular is going to happen, but we can't always be sure what it'll be.

To see what this looks like in practice, we can simply ask for God to fill us, or others, with his Spirit. Some people call this 'prayer ministry', but if that sounds a bit grand, it's just asking God to meet us through this person called the Holy Spirit. Again it's important to say – in case my heavy Thanos emphasis became misleading – that the Spirit is a person not a tool. The Spirit is God, every bit as much as Jesus and the Father are God, and an equal part of the relationship that we have with this mind-bending Trinity.

I don't know if you've ever prayed for someone to receive God's power, but it can be a lot of fun. Sometimes, when we invite the Holy Spirit to meet with someone, they can have a wild and vivid reaction – like when my friend Katie started lurching around on the ground as if she was being controlled from above by a mad puppeteer, or like when a guy I was praying for suddenly started shouting 'I WILL FOLLOW YOU!' in a crowded tent full of 5,000 people who all started staring at us. I think he was talking to God, not me.

Sometimes, though, God's Spirit doesn't provoke a physical reaction at all. Sometimes you can be praying for someone for ages and they barely seem to move at all. This can feel disheartening, especially if you're in the same building as a guy who starts shouting, but the truth is that God can meet just as powerfully with someone in silence as he can in a moment of apparent supernatural chaos. I say this with confidence for two reasons: first, because these big physical reactions never seem to happen to me,* and second because often the most powerful thing the Holy Spirit does is change our hearts.

**If you're the sort of person who never seems to 'experience' God's presence in the same way that others do, I can honestly say that I've barely ever felt anything physical happen when someone has prayed for me – but I have seen dramatic things happen afterwards.*

In the same way, God's power can work in very visible, supernatural ways in front of our eyes, or in quieter actions behind the scenes. My favourite verse in the entire Bible talks about what it feels like to experience being filled with the power of God. It's found in one of Paul's letters to the early Church, in Colossae, and on my *very best days* I recognize what he's talking about. He writes: 'To this end I strenuously contend with all the energy Christ so powerfully works in me' (Colossians 1.29). Paul describes the feeling of the power of God within him as energy coursing through his veins. I don't know if you've ever consumed one of those garishly packaged energy drinks with butch names like 'Sleep Destroyer', after which you can't focus, sit still or maintain eye contact, but I picture something similar. Paul is fizzing with the power of God; it's what propelled him to write all those letters, do a bunch of travelling and frequently pick fights with the people around him.

God promises to give us his Spirit when we ask for it – and as his people we know that this power is always working powerfully within us, whether we 'feel' it physically or not. When we're serving the poor, helping a friend, sharing our faith or sitting quietly in prayer, God is actively involved. Sometimes, though, God goes a step further in allowing us to participate in things that are visibly a bit weird and hard to explain. We sometimes call these things 'spiritual gifts', and we see them talked about quite a bit in the New Testament.

I'm going to resist the strong temptation to assign different-coloured gems to each of the following, but here are just some of the ways in which God's reality-bending power is displayed in the Bible, *and* is also accessible to us today. To be honest, they do unavoidably read like a list of superhero powers . . .

- ***Healing – the power to restore.*** Jesus performed a lot of healings. There are quite a few recorded in the Bible, but one of the Gospels also says that 'Jesus did many other things as well. If every one of them were written down, I suppose that even the whole world would not have room for the books that would be written' (John 21.25). John is probably slightly exaggerating there, but we do know Jesus healed a lot of people, in a lot of different ways. We also know that Jesus said we'd do the same as him and even greater – so it's no surprise that many people experience God's healing today. God often uses his power to bring completely miraculous, medically unexplainable healing – and often he doesn't, too. What we can do is ask for it: and the more often we ask, the more often we'll see him heal.

- ***Prophecy – the power to hear God.*** There are many prophets in the Bible – particularly in the Old Testament – people like

Isaiah, Samuel and Elijah, who heard God's voice on behalf of the people. In the New Testament, Paul encourages us all to have a go at joining that group. He writes (in 1 Corinthians 14.1): 'Follow the way of love and eagerly desire gifts of the Spirit, especially prophecy.' Really simply, this is just about listening to what God is saying and then sharing what we think we've heard with others. There's not much more to it than being quiet, asking God to speak . . . and then trying to stay quiet long enough to give him a chance to do so.* And just like the cultural understanding of prophecy, what God says tends to relate to things that are hidden. Through prophecy, he uncovers things that perhaps we hadn't already realized were true. I don't mean that he'll tell you the sports results in advance, but perhaps he'll enable you to realize something about yourself that you'd never really understood, or give you some guidance about the path that you or others should take.

**This, in my experience, is the hardest bit of prayer. I find it incredibly difficult not to get distracted. I think that's why Paul says we should 'eagerly desire' prophecy – because it takes a pretty superhuman effort of the will not to start thinking about checking your phone when you're faced with a bit of silence.*

- ***Speaking in tongues – the power of connection.*** When Paul writes about the spiritual gifts in his letter to the Corinthians, he quite often mentions the gift of 'speaking in tongues', which is where God's Spirit takes over our speech and enables us to pray in a heavenly language. Sound a bit weird to you? You're absolutely right. But shouldn't the all-consuming power of God feel at least a little bit strange – otherwise how else would we know that it was supernatural? Prayer is incredibly powerful; it causes God to move and to act. But sometimes we just don't know what to pray. When we pray in tongues, the Holy Spirit takes over, helping us to pray in a language we don't understand. In fact we might never get to know exactly what we prayed, unless this gift is used in conjunction with another . . .

- ***Interpretation – the power of understanding.*** The Spirit also gives some people the supernatural ability to make sense of prophetic words or angelic tongues. Where the rest of us might hear a sound a little like an alien from a 1980s straight-to-video film, to someone with the gift of interpretation the tongues make total sense; the interpreter is able to understand the person speaking in tongues as if that person were speaking in the interpreter's own language. In the same way, the Spirit sometimes reveals the meaning of strange-sounding prophecies or dreams to another person. I think the reason that God chooses to work in this way is that it instantly brings the church family together. Instead of giving us gifts as individuals, he gives the gift in two halves, as if to illustrate that he always relates to us as family.

- ***Words of wisdom and knowledge – the power of insight.*** Paul gives us a list of the spiritual gifts in 1 Corinthians 12, and he begins it with this twin reference to 'messages'. These seem to be different from prophecy – which is more about God uncovering or revealing something for us – and instead help us to understand and make sense of things. A 'message of wisdom' could be a better understanding of the Bible, or of who God is; a message of knowledge is an insight into something, or into someone else's life, which we can then share with the person. In both cases, they are things that we couldn't possibly have arrived at without supernatural intervention; without God's help. For example, the Spirit might give you a kind of 'nudge' that your friend really isn't okay, even though on the surface everything seems fine. Or you might find yourself speaking to someone about God, and even as you do you realize that the words are coming from somewhere beyond yourself (this often happens when we take the risk of sharing our faith).

And you know, there's a bunch of other supernatural powers mentioned in the Bible that are presumably also perfectly possible today. My favourite example is the power of teleportation, which happens in the story of Philip and the Ethiopian in Acts 8. The Holy Spirit picks up Philip, who is in the middle of baptizing his new friend, and transports him to another location over 30 miles away. Now, while it's not a commonly seen miracle today, there are quite a few reported instances where people claim that the same thing has happened to them – and who are we to suggest that God *couldn't* choose to do it again? That would be one way to get out of an awkward situation, or a tremendous excuse for missing a school lesson: 'Sorry, Miss, but the Holy Spirit teleported me three towns away.'

*

I don't know how you feel about the idea that God can intervene in the physical world. Maybe you find it all incredibly exciting, and you're about to throw the book down so that you can hit the streets and find some unsuspecting victims to pray for. If you're British like me, you probably feel at least slightly uncomfortable that many of the gifts of the Spirit could cause some slight social embarrassment. But perhaps even more significant than these external manifestations of God's power is the way that it works internally within us, over time.

Have you ever marinated some meat?* The idea is that you coat your steak or chicken breast or whatever in a thick sauce, which over the course of time begins to permeate the meat, so that once you come to cook it, the flavour is enriched. If you marinate for a few minutes, you get a small version of that effect when you come to cook. If you leave it for a couple of hours, the flavour deepens and the meat becomes much tastier. Wait for a day, or in some cases even longer, and you get a total taste explosion when you finally come to eat. In the same way, as we spend time in the presence of God, his power affects and changes us more and more.

**Apologies to vegetarian and vegan readers, but I'm not clear what it is that you guys might marinate. A potato maybe?*

Marinate ourselves a bit in the power of the Holy Spirit and we might start to behave a little more kindly. Spend a few hours more, and we start to take on more of the characteristics of Jesus. When we turn this into a daily practice, however – of asking God to fill us over and again with the power of his Spirit – we start being transformed. And as we experience this transformation in ourselves, God is also equipping us to change the world.

That's why this power – the Holy Spirit – sits in the centre of this list of seven values or attributes. The first three – prayer, worship and family – are about our own metamorphosis into the people God made us to be. The last three – justice, evangelism and creativity – are all about how we then enter into the world as agents of God's kingdom. The Spirit's power sits in the middle because, of course, God is right at the centre of all these things. The Spirit changes us *and* brings change in our world through us.

It's not a video game, though; the amazing thing is that God doesn't wait for us to complete these first three levels before we get to play the rest. He equips us for the adventure of our lives while we're only just starting to navigate it – and what an adventure it is.

7. JUSTICE

On the evening of 6 September 2018, a 26-year-old man named Botham Jean sat watching television in his apartment in Dallas, Texas. He lived on the fourth floor of his building, which had an almost identical floor plan on each level. The resident who lived directly below him on the third floor was 30-year-old police officer Amber Guyger, who was returning home that night at the end of her shift.

Guyger arrived at the door of her apartment to find it slightly ajar – or at least, this was what she later claimed. Concerned that there might be an intruder inside, she drew her gun and entered the darkened living room. She saw a man inside, and instinctively fired at him. He later died from his wound. The man was Botham Jean, and Guyger had accidentally entered the wrong apartment.

A well-liked young man embarking on a promising career as an accountant, killed in the prime of his life. America's widespread gun problem adding yet another death to its awful statistics. And, perhaps to a lesser extent, a police officer's life ruined and career wasted in a single moment. Whatever you think of Guyger – and it's hard to feel great sympathy – she said afterwards: 'I wish he was the one with the gun who had killed me.'

The tragedy of Botham Jean's killing made global news for a couple of reasons. The first concerned the one aspect of this story that I haven't mentioned yet: race. Amber Guyger is white; Botham

Jean was black. If you imagine that this does not have an enormous bearing on what unfolded that night, or how the world responded afterwards, then perhaps you don't know all that much about racial tensions in twenty-first-century America.

If Jean's death had been an isolated incident, then perhaps it would be difficult to draw any wider conclusions. Recent history is littered with examples of incidents involving mainly white police officers and their treatment of mainly black men. Civil rights activists claim that the police are disproportionately brutal, and as in this case trigger-happy, when dealing with black male suspects Men like Michael Brown, gunned down aged 18 in Ferguson, Missouri, after stealing a packet of cigarettes; Eric Garner, strangled to death by an officer's illegal chokehold in Staten Island at 43; Tamir Rice, shot and killed in a park because he'd been seen playing with a toy gun, at *age 12*. All three of these males lost their lives in a single year – 2014 – and their deaths played a part in the launch of the Black Lives Matter movement, which has told their stories, and many like them, ever since.

The point is that these stories always seem to involve black men. There isn't a similarly long list of names of white people who were killed by police because they made a slight move towards their pocket, because in those cases the men tend to be wrestled to the floor rather than shot. By implication, one can speculate that Amber Guyger might not have shot a white man she'd found watching TV in what she thought was her apartment. Now, I know I am massively simplifying an enormously complicated issue that spans hundreds of years of history here, but generally speaking this much is true: the root cause behind the deaths of all these men, and many others like them, is racial injustice.

The police in America are statistically more likely (according to the FBI's own data – the 2012 Supplementary Homicide Report) to kill black people who are not attacking them than white or Hispanic people. There are many explanations for why this happens, but here are a few – and one of them isn't very easy to say. The truth is that there's evidence to suggest that even taking higher arrest rates (and stop and search) into account, black Americans are more likely to commit certain types of crime – including homicide – than people of other races (source: *Channel 4 News* Factcheck, 'Do Black Americans commit more crime?', 2014). The reasons for this are complex, and are heavily influenced by the increased levels of poverty and social deprivation faced by many black people, which drives some to believe they have no other option than to turn to crime. But it is true. So, if you're a police officer, you are more likely to fear or suspect an average black male than an average white one.

Meanwhile, American culture – TV, music and film – frequently portrays black men as violent and aggressive; gun-toting, even. Not only that, but the whole nation is still barely 50 years on from a period in history where black people were legally treated as second-class citizens. All of these factors – poverty, media, history, crime – work together to create a backdrop to which police officers are not immune. When they see a black man, they are instinctively influenced by all of this gentle (or more severe) prejudice. This is no defence of police brutality, but the police don't just choose to display racial injustice; they have to actively choose not to, because the entire system that they are part of is unjust.

America – no, the entire Western world – has a problem with racial injustice. Largely because of the horrific legacy of slavery, through which African natives were captured, dehumanized and forced to work for their white masters across hundreds of years, a gigantic rift has been created in our culture which means that – even though slavery itself has been outlawed in most countries for almost a hundred years – black and white people do not in general enter the world on a level playing field. The world is racially unjust.

When Amber Guyger entered the apartment and saw Botham Jean, she proved that injustice in the split-second of thought-processing time that it took to pull the trigger. Many were horrified, others became angry. Some black people no doubt became even more hardened in their dislike and mistrust of the white police; others leapt to Guyger's defence and argued that she was right to shoot. In the end, Jean and Guyger just became another two players in a broken system that cycles around and around. Neither his death nor her conviction will break that cycle; something far greater is needed to do that.

*

What is justice? It's a strange word, because it's one that is perhaps easier to define in terms of its absence. We're so familiar with what *in*justice looks like that it can be harder to imagine things actually being right. But that's what justice is in essence: things being right, fair, as they were originally intended; justice is the world *as it should be*.

We all know, however, that the world is not always like this. Racial injustice is just one way in which we see the inequality, the brokenness of our world, but we could have begun by looking through so many other lenses. Here are a few more:

- **Poverty**, and the many root causes behind it, which means that around 700 million people around the world live on less than US$1.90 a day (source: World Bank). Although that number has fallen sharply from nearly 2 billion in 1990, that is mainly because of economic growth in massive countries such as China and India. Poverty in Sub-Saharan Africa is actually projected to increase – and every country in the world still carries some reflection of the bigger picture: a few people horde most of the wealth, and at the other end of society many people have almost nothing. There are always many factors involved, but the largest is simply where someone was born. You could arrive in the world into a wealthy family with a second house by the beach, or into a Brazilian *favela*: either way, the chances are that you'll stay there.

- **Gender-related injustice**, including sexism. Despite some advancements in recent years, we are all still living with the legacy of hundreds of years of living in male-dominated societies. Until a few decades ago, the majority of people still believed that a woman's place is in the home, and the numbers of women now running the biggest companies prove that not many are yet finding their place in the boardroom. The vast majority of sexual violence and harassment is committed by men against women – and thanks to the #metoo movement we're now realizing this is a much more widespread problem than some of us ever knew. Meanwhile pornography – which secretly passes through the laptops and smartphones of billions of people around the world – continues to reinforce sexualizing, dehumanizing ideas about women. In some countries, these are comparatively trivial concerns compared to issues such as forced marriage and female genital mutilation. The way our world treats men and women is not the same; it is not equal or fair.

- **Climate injustice**, and what happens to our world when we don't look after it properly. Whatever you think about the various species of weird-looking sea creatures that are being wiped out by our unsustainable approach to burning off the world's resources, there are two significant and enormous groups of people who are being affected every time the polar ice caps retract a little further, or that pollution count inches higher. The first are all the people living today in areas that are damaged by climate change: farmers in parts of South Asia whose crop harvests are being devastated by flooding; people in South America whose environments are changing from tropical forest into savannah. The second are the generations who will inherit this planet and ask why they are experiencing a decreasing quality of life. The way that the world uses resources today, in order to carry on living in the way in which we've become accustomed, is unjust, and sadly by the time this becomes obvious to all of us it will be too late to stop the devastating effects.

- **Modern-day slavery**, which unthinkably means an estimated 40 million people worldwide are forced to work against their will, a quarter of them children. Not only that, but a huge subsection of these are used as sexual slaves: women, girls and boys imprisoned and raped multiple times each day by people paying a slave-owner to do so. Others are taken from their homes and trained as child soldiers, brutalized to commit heinous acts on behalf of their captors. We like to believe that we have eliminated slavery from our civilized societies; in fact, slaves are everywhere, including the most developed nations on earth.

There are many other examples of prejudice, inequality and rank unfairness in our world today. **Homophobia**, which in some countries means men and women are still executed because of who they have fallen in love with. **Ableism**, which can mean that those with disabilities or additional needs are – silently or blatantly – marginalized, ignored or even abused. **Ageism**, which works both ways – demonizing the young and treating the eldery as if they are a burden. **Human rights abuses**, which can lead to men, women and children being imprisoned because of their beliefs. The list goes on and on.

*

What does God think about all this? And why, given all the power we talked about in the last chapter, doesn't he stop it?

First of all, the Bible tells us that God sees the injustice on earth, and it makes him angry. Like, seriously furious. Proverbs 6 says that 'hands that shed innocent blood' are 'an abomination to the Lord'. In fact, it's one of the rare times in the Bible that we actually hear the language of 'hate' rather than love. God is brimming with rage at those who perpetrate injustice, and that's not because he's got an angry temperament. But every victim of injustice is God's precious child, and he cares for each one of them with a love so great that we can't even fathom it. He cares so much about justice for his people that some scholars argue that over 2,000 verses in the Bible focus on the issue. There are constant references in the Old Testament to caring for the poor and needy, to looking after the orphan and the widow and anyone who has been a victim of someone else's bad decisions.

So then God is not only angry, but compassionate. He feels the pain of those who suffer injustice. I believe – since God's character is revealed through Jesus who wept over the death of a friend – that God isn't just angry about injustice, he's also devastated by it. His deep love for us causes him to feel an agonizing pain when we are hurt. He suffers with us.

So again you might ask, why doesn't he do anything about it?

But of course, he has done something about it. Something spectacular that has the power to disarm injustice once and for all, and to renew everything so that it can finally get to its rightful state. He sent his Son to die.

All these injustices and more have been around for thousands of years. And all of them, right at the heart, have the same ugly root cause: selfishness. The desire to put ourselves first, and to put others beneath us; the desire to have what we want, even if it means others go without. In essence, it's us making ourselves into the god of our lives; putting ourselves at the centre (sound familiar?). This is what sin is, and that's what Jesus came to defeat.

Sin isn't just about a few individual people making selfish choices. Sin grows from there into systems of oppression. Imagine a fictional country made up of farmlands, on which live a group of farmers with blonde hair and a group with brown hair. The blondes get together one day and decide to take over all the farmlands, and to drive the brown-hairs into one corner of the nation. They beat them up and take all their tools too, and make them live off the scraps of their own feasting. So for generations afterwards, the blonde families own and harvest all the land, and the rest live destitute on the margins. And what's worse is that years later, no one really understands how it started; no one can imagine a way to turn things back to how they were meant to be. This is how sin works: it grows from personal decisions into communal oppression – and it's incredibly hard to break the power of a whole system.

When Jesus came to the earth, he announced that 'The kingdom of God has come near' (Mark 1.15). That's because he was going to challenge people not only to deal with their personal issues, but also to deal with top-level change. Jesus came to challenge the systems that have all become broken by sin; by human beings putting themselves first, making themselves God. By dying on the cross, he broke the power of sin itself – meaning that sin no longer separates us from God. He made the restoration of the world possible; because of the cross, things can now become as they were always meant to be.

Before he died, though, Jesus spent three years explaining the idea of a better world to his followers. He talked about this idea of the kingdom – where God is in his rightful place at the heart of all things – more than anything else. It's as if he walked into that fictional farm country and explained what it would look like to turn the clock back; to get back to how things were before sin took a hold.

Jesus did what no one else could do – he stopped the world from sliding on and on into eternal disaster. But he recruits us, his followers, to be part of what comes next: the advance of the kingdom. And when the kingdom of God advances, injustice begins to retreat. Suddenly, through Jesus' emergence, there's a spark of rebellion – a chance that the light could overcome the darkness after all, against the odds. The evil systems that seem to almost overwhelm the world could yet be overthrown.

So maybe we shouldn't ask: why isn't God solving the problem of injustice? Maybe a better question is: how do I become part of his solution?

As a follower of Jesus, you are invited to participate in that rebellion against sin. We overthrow one kingdom by bringing in another. If we're serious about being a part of that, it's going to involve some action on our part. Start the cool 1980s Saturday teatime TV show music,* it's time to get real.

**If you have no idea what I'm talking about, when I was young there were some amazing low-budget action series that always, always had a killer theme tune.*

- ***Step 1: Self-reflect.*** I know it doesn't sound very dynamic as a starting point, but if you're going to try to stand up against injustice, you need to know where you might be part of the problem. Think about where in your life you might, even without knowing it, be part of the oppression of others. How do your purchasing choices, or the way you treat other people, contribute to some of these problems? Jesus taught (in Matthew 7.5) that before we point out the speck of sawdust in someone else's eye, it's good to acknowledge the plank of wood in our own. This might involve making some changes – for instance in how you spend your money – before you even begin.

- ***Step 2: Pray.*** That's right – you might be a great justice-avenger in the making, but you'll do a much better job with God's help. Ask him to give you eyes to see the things around you that need to change, and the ways you might be able to make a difference. All the great Christian justice warriors – from William Wilberforce to Nelson Mandela – spent enormous amounts of time in prayer before they sought to take on the world, and Jesus did the same. Those aren't bad role models to follow.

- ***Step 3: Focus down.*** You can't change everything, all at once, and Jesus isn't asking you to. But perhaps it is possible to focus on one injustice, one thing that you really want to see change, and then make a concerted effort to make a difference in that area. No one apart from Jesus has ever fought all the broken systems of the world at once, so best be specific about what you could do.

- ***Step 4: Get educated.*** You can't change something that you don't understand. So if you care about something, read up on it. You don't need to consume vast academic volumes, but you should at least have searched the internet enough to know what you're talking about. Problems are always more complicated than they first appear. As part of this, it's good to find out what others are already doing in the area you care about. There are over 185,000 registered charities in the UK alone, all trying to make the world a better place; it's likely that there are people like you, already doing what you want to do, just waiting for people to join them.

- ***Step 5: Get approximate.*** One of my personal heroes is Bryan Stevenson, the Christ-following lawyer played by Michael B. Jordan in the film *Just Mercy*, who has been responsible for overturning countless unjust cases against men on Death Row. I had the privilege of hearing Bryan in conversation with another one of my heroes, Archbishop Justin Welby, a few years ago,* when he was asked about how we bring real change in a world of injustice.

  **Just to be clear, they were talking in front of an audience. It wasn't as if I was hiding under the Archbishop's dinner table or something.*

  His first response was that 'we have to get approximate to the problems we care about'. You can't really change things if you're always going to maintain a safe distance from them. Mother Teresa didn't alleviate poverty by making YouTube messages to encourage the poor – she got eye to eye with them and started to serve. This may not be completely practical for you right now, but there are still ways in which you can increase your proximity to the issue you're trying to change. If you want to challenge homophobia, it might be wise to speak to some of the people who face it, rather than just assuming how they might feel and speaking for them.

- ***Step 6: Take prophetic action.*** Ask God's Holy Spirit to empower you to act. Whether that's in an incredibly visible way like launching a local campaign, or through an unseen but persistent activity like writing letters to persecuted Christians, it doesn't really matter. Every action against injustice chips a little more paint off our broken world, and brings the glory of the kingdom just a fraction further into view.

God cares passionately about injustice. His long-term solution for ending it is the advance of his kingdom. Part of being his people – part of putting him at the centre of our lives – is joining in with the sometimes-painful, often-meaningful adventure of that mission. Because when we choose to practise the way of Jesus in a world that knows deep down it's broken, incredible things can start to happen.

*

In September 2019, just over a year after Botham Jean was killed, the trial of Amber Guyger began. Guyger did not deny the events of that tragic night. In fact she said, 'I hate myself every single day' for what had happened. While her lawyers aimed for a lower verdict of manslaughter, she was convicted of murder and sentenced to ten years in prison. The outcome stirred up anger and hatred on every side, social media proving an ugly cauldron of public opinion.

Then, at the very end of the case, something remarkable happened. Following sentencing, Jean's 18-year-old younger brother Brandt took the stand to address Guyger directly. You might expect that given this opportunity the young man would fire a few carefully rehearsed words of fury and hatred toward his brother's killer, to torment her as she lay awake at night in prison. Instead, this is a direct transcript of what he said:

> If you truly are sorry, I know I can speak for myself, I forgive you. And I know if you go to God and ask him, he will forgive you.
>
> And I don't think anyone can say it – again I'm speaking for myself and not on behalf of my family – but I love you just like anyone else.

Isn't that extraordinary? Brandt Jean – like his brother and the rest of his family – is a churchgoing Christian. But to talk about forgiveness and love like that, in a moment like that – even for a Christian this seems remarkable. And then he went even further:

> And I'm not going to say I hope you rot and die, just like my brother did, but I personally want the best for you. And I wasn't going to ever say this in front of my family or anyone, but I don't even want you to go to jail. I want the best for you, because I know that's exactly what Botham would want you to do. And the best would be: give your life to Christ. I'm not going to say anything else. I think giving your life to Christ would be the best thing that Botham would want you to do.
>
> Again, I love you as a person. And I don't wish anything bad on you.
>
> I don't know if this is possible, but can I give her a hug, please? Please?

I haven't added a single word to what Brandt Jean said that day. The judge, who also happened to be African-American and a Christian, allowed him his final request, and the pair hugged tearfully in the centre of the courtroom. For a few moments, the system of racial injustice and the power of sin itself were completely disabled by grace.

Guyger must still face justice, and the titanic problem of racism in America hasn't been dismantled by a single incident of forgiveness. Setting the story to emotive music and turning it into a viral video shouldn't ease our discomfort at Botham Jean's murder, nor should it mislead us to believe that his family should ever have been put in this position in the first place. His death was an outrage, and yet another chapter in an outrageous story that must be told over and over again. This is what happens in a system of injustice and sin.

But what Brandt Jean did, in that moment, was quite incredible. Most of us would have understood if he'd chosen to pour hatred and anger on top of tragedy and murder. He didn't; he chose to bring faith, hope and love instead. These are the ways of the kingdom of God, and it is only through practising them that we will truly see an end to injustice.

8.
EVANGELISM

There are some words in the English language that provoke an immediate reaction in most people. There are a few quite obvious ones, which I won't mention here, but then there are others that – generally speaking – cause an exaggerated response in one direction or another. You either love that thing or you hate it. Examples include: fishing, haggis and Justin Bieber. Not only does the naming of these lead to extreme reactions, but the people who love them generally won't stop there; they're on a mission to persuade the world that the thing they love should be loved by all. They want to get the haggis haters to try a bite; they want the music snobs to at least *listen* to 'Baby', feat. Ludacris.

Another such word is 'cricket'. Few people in my experience feel completely neutral about it. You either love it or you hate it, and if you hate it . . . let me explain to you just how wrong you are. Cricket – at the very highest level – is a sport played by two teams of elite athletes who have trained their entire lives for this. While the village version you might have strolled past is often fairly gentle and sedate, at international level the sport is positively gladiatorial. In the middle of the field stands a man (women's cricket is also available), partly padded but still hugely exposed to the vicious attack he's about to face. In his hands he holds a small piece of English willow, shaped into a bat, with which he somehow has to drive a ball past 11 strategically placed opponents. At the same time, he also has to guard a collection of wooden objects behind him (which are larger than the bat). One of the players runs at him with wild fury in his eyes and unleashes a spherical missile in his direction from 22 yards away, at a speed approaching *100 miles per hour*. What this means is that the batsman has approximately half a second in which to: see the ball, work out where it's going, choose a shot to try to play in response *and* successfully execute it.

If he fails, the wooden objects behind him are splintered and his contribution is over. If he succeeds, he's only got a few moments to prepare to face the same thing again.

The contest between these two highly skilled sportspeople is the very heart of cricket. It is however only the centrepiece of a very large and multi-layered sporting onion. Beyond the basic battle between bat and ball it is a game of intense and complex strategy, as mentally taxing as chess and as physically demanding as a long-distance race. Players must maintain focus and concentration for days on end, always waiting for the rare moment when they or their opponent makes a mistake. Meanwhile for fans, it is a game that rewards immersion; a world of stories and statistics that will go on for ever if you'll let it.

You get the picture: cricket is a game I love. Not only that, but I believe that the people who don't get cricket, or think that they hate it, simply don't understand how wonderful it is. I am always on a mission to encourage just a few more people to taste and see how good the sport is, constantly pleading with them just to give it a chance. Because, deep down, I have a conviction that everyone would enjoy the game if they only knew it like I do.

Of course, I know that's not true. I understand that some people will never love cricket, even if they are forcibly made to play it for years (sorry, Saunders kids). Hopefully, though, this provides a good example of what it means to feel and act *evangelistically* about something, because that's what we're going to look at next.

*

Evangelism is dictionary-defined as 'zealous advocacy or support of a particular cause'. It's when we believe in the rightness of something so much that we cannot fail to talk about it to others. In fact we don't just talk about it, we desperately and passionately try to persuade people who don't currently share our view that they should change their minds and subscribe to it. We see this all the time in politics, when rosette-wearing campaigners arrive on your doorstep to convince you that their particular party isn't actually as evil as you think. We see it on social media, as fans of a particular band or TV series or brand of stationery unleash a persistent stream of spam messages about why you should love that thing too. Major tech companies such as Apple and Google employ people called 'technology evangelists' whose job it is to convince people to adopt and use new products.

As followers of Jesus, evangelism should probably come fairly naturally to us. If we understand and believe the central message of Christianity it makes sense that we'd want to share that. If we believe we know the meaning of life itself, why wouldn't we tell as many people as possible what it is?

Jesus seems to agree. After he's been raised from the dead, he gathers his followers and gives them a really clear final instruction. These aren't quite his last words (the actual last thing he does is promise the Holy Spirit), but they're definitely part of his closing comments:

> 'All authority in heaven and on earth has been given to me. Therefore go and make disciples of all nations, baptising them

> in the name of the Father and of the Son and of the Holy Spirit, and teaching them to obey everything I have commanded you. And surely I am with you always, to the very end of the age.' (Matthew 28.18–20)

Jesus tells the Church to 'go and make disciples' all over the earth. In other words: 'Invite people to follow me, just as you have followed me. Don't keep this good news to yourself, but share it with others, and what's more help them to put it into practical action in their lives too.' This isn't part of a long list of instructions where you can opt into the bits you like; this is the climactic command from Jesus to the Church. Evangelism is one of the primary jobs that he gives to us.

To recap, then: it makes sense to us that we would want to share the good news about Jesus with the world, and the Bible seems pretty clear that this is what we're meant to do. So then . . . why does it feel so very difficult?

I was not a popular kid at school. I've already explained that I was a chubby, cricket-loving *Doctor Who* fanatic, and my conversion to Christianity at age 14 didn't exactly help me to increase my credibility. When I became a follower of Jesus I instinctively knew that everything I'd been denying and pushing away up till then was completely true. It was as if I'd been irrationally refusing to eat Indian food for the whole of my life, before finally taking a bite and realizing instantly that it was the cuisine of heaven. Yet just because I knew that God was real, and that fulfilment and meaning for me and others would only be found in relationship with him, that didn't make it any easier for me to tell those other people about him. From the start, my youth leaders explained the whole 'go and make disciples' element of Christianity, but honestly I didn't believe most of the people in my school would follow a film recommendation from me, let alone a religious one.*

**Incidentally, I had a reputation then for always choosing terrible films.*

I did try. I made fumbling attempts to convince some of my classmates that they should give church a try, or at least come to youth group, where it was possible to meet girls. For the most part they declined, not very politely, but over the course of several years one or two followed me into the strange world of 1990s Evangelical Christianity. When I decided to get baptized – the Christian ritual of being totally immersed in water to symbolize new life in Jesus – many of my classmates came out of a sense of intrigue. They made a lot of cruel jokes about how much water would be left in the pool after my ample body had displaced it all, but they came and they at least partly listened.

The point is: we all get how strange and difficult evangelism is. Not only are you trying to convince someone else of your point of view – and everyone knows how that usually goes – but you're also asking them to consider shifting their position on one of the most primal of beliefs: the existence of God. It's not as if you're trying to persuade someone to switch to light mayonnaise because it tastes just as good. By even listening to you, they're allowing you to challenge something about which they may hold a very strong opinion. At best, they might brush you off; at worst, they might bite back hard.

There's a big but, though. If evangelism in its simplest form is walking across a room or a playground or an office and telling someone about our faith in Jesus, then we should never imagine that we do this alone.

Here's something that I once heard from a wise man named Rico.* When you speak to your friend about Jesus, Jesus' promise that 'I am with you always' comes into very sharp effect. Imagine it like this: even as you're telling the other person that you believe in God, and that you think faith in Jesus could be the answer they're looking for too, the Holy Spirit is there also. Not just standing around being mysterious and invisible, but whispering into that person's ear: 'This is true . . . this is true . . . this is true.'

**I tell you his name, because he's the only person I know who is called this who isn't one of the penguins in* Penguins of Madagascar.

When I made that decision to stop being stubborn and listen to the person who first told me about Jesus, I experienced exactly that. It was as if something made the wall of certainty that I'd previously had melt away. God took their bravery in stepping out to talk about him, and then supernaturally multiplied the power of that moment. I knew it was true because God changed my heart.

Ultimately, we don't convince anyone to follow Jesus. God invites us into and chooses to use us as part of the process, but in the end he's always the one who calls out, 'Come, follow me.' As painful as this might feel for our own ego, whether or not someone chooses to respond is down to them – and God.

We keep on making the case, though, and not just because Jesus commanded it. We also talk to our friends about our faith because we can see how good it would be for them. For the friend who is lonely, or lacking direction, or caught up in ultimately fruitless ambition, or struggling, or confused about who they even are, we who follow Jesus can see that he's the greatest possible answer. We know that transformation comes – sometimes slowly and over time – through knowing and following him.

That's why we keep on plucking up the courage, even though we've been knocked back, laughed at or had our head bitten off before. Evangelism shouldn't be driven by a desire to win the argument or to have other people concede that we are right. Evangelism is propelled by deep love for our friends; by a desire for them not to miss out on the meaning, comfort, purpose and adventure that we experience in knowing God. We simply want them to be part of the family, because we know that's the best place for them.

*

There are a lot of ways to 'walk across a room', so to speak. We don't necessarily have to ask someone to stop what they're doing and look us directly in the eyes while we talk them through the major events of the Bible (also, don't do this, it sounds a bit weird); that's not all that qualifies as evangelism. The first step in making a new disciple might look like any number of things. Here are a few examples (see which sound most appealing to you):

- ***Issuing an invitation.*** You simply ask someone if they'd like to come along to an event which might give them a positive experience of Christian community. That might be a church service, a youth group, a bowling trip or a meal at a friend's house. Anything that brings them into a positive relationship with the family of God is a good and helpful thing.

- ***Being honest about your faith.*** The Bible talks about not hiding our light (Matthew 5.15–16) but instead letting it 'shine before others'. It may be tempting to keep our faith quiet, but by doing that we deprive others of the chance to see how God is helping and changing us. I'm not suggesting you put up a 40-foot banner outside your house that says, 'Hey everyone, I FOUND GOD', but at least make sure that your friends know. Try telling them in a matter-of-fact way. Then, when they find they have questions about faith, they are more likely to come to you with them.

- ***Sharing on social media.*** We all know how daunting it can feel to make ourselves vulnerable on social media, and you don't have to replace your usual grinning selfies with paintings of Jesus. But there are ways to gently let people know that you're part of a church community, or that faith is important to you, without coming across as if you've joined a weird cult. Sometimes, there's even the natural opportunity to share an encouraging quote or video with your friends. People love that stuff.

- ***Offering to pray.*** Many people find the idea of prayer comforting, even if they don't really believe in God. If you know someone who is going through something tough, it isn't terribly offensive to tell them that they'll be in your prayers, or even to ask if you can pray for them. Be prepared for rejection of course, but don't let that stop you offering; even those who say 'no' may feel touched by the offer.

Any of these simple acts could lead someone to take another step towards Jesus. And the chances are that you will eventually find yourself in an actual conversation with someone about what it means to follow him. Which raises the important question: what do you do when you find yourself in a conversation about faith?

Read the situation. If a friend (or indeed, an enemy) talks to you about your faith, you should always make sure you're really paying attention to where they're coming from. Your friend may just want to get to know you a little better, and so is finding out a bit more about what makes you tick. There's a big difference, for example, between your friend responding to something you've said with 'That's interesting', and your friend saying '*I'm interested*'. The journey of leading someone towards Jesus can be long and winding, and it might just begin with a gentle conversation; two friends getting a bit more real with each other.

Pray while you're listening. Sure, this can feel like a tricky/scary moment. So ask God for his help, and invite him to guide the conversation. Two things you can be sure of at this point: he's present with you in this; and he's absolutely loving it.

Listen to them first. People tend to be much more open to hearing what you have to say when they know you're interested in listening to them too. If you're in a conversation about God, ask your friend about the journey that has led them up to this conversation. And don't just do this to get it out of the way so that you can share your important message – you may learn something amazing about someone, or notice something they're saying that suggests God has already been working in their life. The Holy Spirit is with you – and will help you to hear what they're *really* saying, beyond just the words they speak.

Don't overwhelm. So perhaps the person is actually interested in understanding what the whole deal is with Jesus. That's great! Do not now feel that it is your responsibility to condense the entire Bible into nine succinct sentences delivered in a single breath.* You don't need to hit people over the head with endless stories about why you're right, or how great Jesus is. Most importantly of all, you must not view this one conversation as your only chance to make your friend turn into a Christian. Most people who make that decision do so over a journey of many steps – this chat might be just one of them.

**When I was 16, I made my friend Mark walk around the block over and over again while I explained every bit of Christianity that I knew in a frantic voice, before I let him get a single word in. He did not become a follower of Jesus that day.*

Share the gospel simply. The beauty of the Christian faith is that it is deep enough for people to spend an entire lifetime studying, and simple enough that a small child can understand it. At the very heart is the most beautiful and easy-to-understand idea: there is a God, and he loves you. If you are able to get those words out, then you have already followed Jesus' command. There's more to say, but that might be enough for one day.

If you don't know the answer, say so. In 1 Peter 3.15, the author writes: 'Always be prepared to give an answer to everyone who asks you to give the reason for the hope that you have.' That means we should actively try to prepare for conversations like the one I'm describing, and the way we do that is by thinking through the big questions for ourselves. Some questions are really difficult, though, and you definitely don't get extra evangelism points for trying to con your way through them. If a friend asks you a hard question – such as, 'Why does God allow suffering?', 'What truth is there in other religions?' or, 'If God is good, why did they cancel *Firefly*?' – then simply promise to go away, think, read and ask others about it, and then return. It is very important that you do then come back rather than run away, hide and hope they'll forget.

Don't skip the tricky bits. The overwhelming message of Christianity is that God loves us. But in the Bible, when Jesus invites us to know and believe in him, he also tells us to 'repent'. Repentance is simply agreeing to turn around from your present direction, as you would in a car that is in danger of veering off a cliff, and to head back to the route that was always intended for you. It's simply saying to God, 'I'm sorry I've lived my own way and tried to live without you – I don't want to do that any more.' We all know, deep down, that this is a hard thing to say, but also that it is beautifully right. If we leave this out of our explanation of what following Jesus is, then we've not given our friends the full picture. Jesus can only transform us when we agree to leave our existing life and switch our allegiance to him.

Do it with love, not to win. Ultimately, we share the good news about Jesus with our friends because we love them, and because we know that getting to know Jesus, and becoming part of his family, is the best thing that could happen to them. We don't do it because we want to be proved right. The writer Philip Yancey once said that 'no one ever converted to Christianity because they lost the argument'. It's true: your friend will ultimately make their own decision to respond to God's voice – all you can do is be a friend, holding a torch, helping to illuminate the path.

Don't force it, but you can lead someone to Jesus. The vast majority of 'evangelistic' conversations do not end in someone becoming a Christian. Ninety-nine per cent of them don't – most are just another stepping-stone in the journey. My friend Steven told me that he'd once heard about this explained in terms of the non-existence of constipated trees. As in, you never see a tree straining to do what comes naturally. This is a weird image, but I like it. We shouldn't try to force the issue.

Occasionally, though, you might find yourself in a situation where someone says: 'Yes, I want to become a Christian.'* If this happens, do not panic. Again, this is not really something that you can get badly wrong, and if you've got to this point you can be confident that the Holy Spirit is basically in charge anyway.

**It's unlikely they'll say these words exactly.*

Simply ask your friend if they'll pray with you, and then ask Jesus to come into their life. It's quite a good thing, if they don't find it strange, to invite them to repeat your words after you. Ask that you will both receive God's love and his Spirit; say sorry for the times that you've gone your own way. Pledge your future to Jesus. Receive the incredible hope of eternal life. That's it.

*

One of the most incredible things about following Jesus is realizing that he wants to use us in the world. Even though he has the power to do anything he wants, he empowers the Church that he loves so much to be his hands and feet. He uses us to be a part of putting right the things that have gone wrong, as we saw in the last chapter, and he invites us to play a major part in remaking the world as it should be – as we'll see in the next one.

Part of the adventure is helping the family to grow. The message of Jesus started among a rag-tag bunch of first-century nobodies and grew into a global movement with 2 billion members. God did that through his Church; we are the new generations of that movement.

The people all around you, who don't know Jesus, will have their lives utterly turned upside down for the better when they do. By choosing to follow him, they will find meaning that they never thought possible in this life, and the certain promise that death will not be the end. Yet they may never know that Christianity is any more than a weird character trait unless they witness it at work in someone they know and trust. And that means the best person who could possibly reach your friends with this incredible message . . . is you.

9.
CREATIVITY

Who doesn't like making top-ten lists? The chance to reflect on your favourite games, or books, movies, albums or TV shows. It's always a joy to remember those little highlights of culture that stand head and shoulders above the rest – for you at least. That's the brilliant thing about the creative arts: everyone loves slightly different things, and everything is loved by someone. You can see a piece of art that looks like two splodges of red paint on a brown wall and to someone else it seems to be a masterpiece. You love an album so much that you listen to it on repeat for three days, and your friend can't get past the first two tracks. Everyone's top ten is slightly different.

Pick your favourite field of the arts – TV perhaps, music, film, whatever – and spend a couple of minutes trying to think through your top ten in that area. Maybe even write it down, unless your list is so embarrassing that you'd be mortified if anyone ever found it.*

**It's okay to love the Famous Five books but prefer everyone to think that you really love* The Hunger Games. *By the way, that would make for an awesome crossover series.*

Once you've made your list, look or think over it. The creative arts – those things that others have made to entertain, inspire and challenge us – are a massive source of happiness and meaning for us, partly because there is so much diversity within them. It might be that the ten books that have changed your life are all science fiction novels, but it's more likely that there's a broader range than that.

Your list of the greatest Xbox games ever might all involve running around shooting people online, but I'll bet that it's more likely to be a mix of genres and styles. One of the most exciting things about art is that when you put it through the filter of human artists, it splits off in a million different directions.

Now let me ask you something: what is it that unites everything on your list – no matter how diverse or radical the things you wrote down? The answer is the creative spark, experienced an incalculable number of times, in every different way imaginable, by people all over the world. Every work of art, performance and ingenuity that you've ever known and loved – as well as all things that you didn't understand or enjoy – all have that same common root of human creativity. And where does creativity come from? Come on, we're nine chapters in; I think you know where we're going here . . .

*

The first thing that happens in the Bible is that *God creates*. Those are literally the first five words of the book: *'In the beginning God created'*. The universe is formless and empty, and God unleashes the full force of his unparalleled, indescribable creative power upon it. Galaxies burst into life; stars and planets and moons take shape. Light blazes; elements form. And centre stage, to us at least, the world we live in begins to grow and flourish. Over the period of creation,* the most awesome and constant string of inventions and innovations in history is released into the earth. Mountains. Lions. Diamonds. Clouds.

**Could have been seven actual days. Probably wasn't.*

At the end of the creation story, in Genesis 1, God is talking to himself – which if you were paying attention during Chapter 6, isn't weird at all – and he says something unbelievably significant to our understanding of who we are:

> Then God said, 'Let us make mankind in our image, in our likeness, so that they may rule over the fish in the sea and the birds in the sky, over the livestock and all the wild animals, and over all the creatures that move along the ground.' So God created mankind in his own image, in the image of God he created them; male and female he created them.
> (Genesis 1.26–27)

The final step of God's great creative process was to create women and men. And as he did so, he somehow made them 'in his own image', perhaps not literally to look like him, but to be like little representations of him: small versions, not God but like him. And that wasn't just about their appearance, but about who they were. They were created to live in community, just like God. They were created to take care of creation, just like God. They were infused with the attributes of God himself: love, care, compassion . . . and creativity. In the very next verse he invites them literally to get creative – in the reproductive sense – but less than a chapter later he begins to draw creativity out of them, inviting Adam to come up with names for all the animals.*

**I guess that's why we have creatures called the tasselled wobbegong and the spiny lumpsucker.*

If you have ever found yourself saying the words 'I'm not creative', then you're wrong. You were formed in the image of the most creative being in the universe, and you carry his creative spark. We all do – the directors of the greatest films in history, and the team behind the worst novelty rap song ever recorded; the great novelists, and the artists who've never sold a single painting. In fact, that God-given creativity reaches far beyond the arts; every genius entrepreneur, pioneering scientist, quick-thinking sportsperson and great political thinker carries and makes use of that awesome divine gift. So do all the people who enter those disciplines and never reach levels of recognition or 'success'. God's creativity flows through all of us. The question is: what are we going to do with it?

*

Throughout this book I've often talked about the 'adventure' of following Jesus. I honestly believe that everything we've looked at so far is another rich part of an incredible journey. If that was *all* we were invited to spend our lives doing, then it would be more than enough. But here's one more thing to consider: what does it mean for us to actively engage our creative gifts in this adventure of being part of God's family?

You may already have a good idea of what your creative gifts are. You might be a musician or a poet, or that person who always has new ideas; or you might be a born engineer, or a painter, or basketball-crazy. It might be that you're still in the process of trying a few things out, to see what makes you really come alive. Whatever it is that you do best – or enjoy most – it's easy to accidentally leave God out of the picture. We can easily fall into the trap of thinking that God isn't interested in our time on the tennis court, or writing that business plan, or strumming those chords. And, of course, billions of people around the world, all of them infused with the divine creative spark, do that every day.

As followers of Jesus, though, we miss out on so much by doing that. We miss the chance to bump into God in so many more moments and situations, and perhaps we even miss out on better understanding who we are as the image-bearers of God. Because God is *profoundly* interested in the things we think and create and do. He's running alongside us when we make that mazy run along the hockey pitch; he's sitting next to us in the practice room when we play that last note wrong on the eighteenth try. He has filled us with creativity and offered us a lifetime to explore it – which means, even if you don't know it now, you might one day write a prize-winning novel, or invent a widget that transforms the way we live, or help to cure cancer, or paint a masterpiece.

I believe that even if we don't hit acclaimed levels of creativity, God still wants us to discover and explore the creative spark within us, and he wants us to include him in it all. God's deep desire is to be in a relationship with his children *all the time*, and he never, ever gets tired of being with us as we think, dream, work and play. He created you with all your passions and interests, and he wants to spend time with you as you enjoy them. In a small way, I get to experience this with my own children. I love watching my kids practising musical instruments, or playing sport, or coming up with endless quizzes, or whatever it is they're currently obsessed with.* But do you know what I've realized? They love me being there too. They love the fact that their dad is watching them try something different, improve at it, maybe even succeed. When my nine-year-old son Samuel scores a goal for his football team he celebrates with his friends, but he always, *always* gives a quick glance in my direction to make sure I saw it. He loves to share his creative gifts with his dad; perhaps that's the most natural, obvious and beautiful thing.

**At the time of writing: inventing dinosaurs, colouring flags, making World's Strongest Man Top Trumps and watching a competitive dog show called Crufts. Kids are weird.*

But this is a pale imitation of how it can be between us and God. Our heavenly Father loves it when we involve him in our passions and our ideas – he literally can't get enough of them. And even more than that, I think he always wants to make use of those things, sometimes in ways that we would never have imagined. God wants to be a part of our music, our science, our sport, our business and everything else. When we realize that, an awesome opportunity opens up to go into partnership with him. Part of the joy of following Jesus is learning to put our creativity to work for him in the world.

*

Having started this chapter on the very first page of the Bible, we're now going to skip to the end and return to a passage we've already visited once (in Chapter 2). In it the apostle John is receiving a vision from God about what will happen when the kingdom of God begins to fully break out. If you'll remember, he says this: 'He who was seated on the throne said, "I am making everything new"' (Revelation 21.5).

The very start and the very end of the Bible both talk about the incredible creativity of God. He is the fountain from which all creativity flows – both in the original creation of the world and then in its re-creation. But notice that he doesn't say, 'I have *made* everything new.' He doesn't speak it all into being, like he did the first time around. Now it's a process – a gradual re-making – and the reason why is that this time he's not doing it on his own.

God's kingdom – the way things are meant to be – is slowly but surely emerging in our world. It doesn't happen overnight; we don't suddenly see all the pain and suffering and other bad stuff disappear to be replaced by instant perfection. Instead, God invites us to be part of his grand project to reimagine, rebuild and repaint the world over time.

Now, try to think of your creative gifts through that lens. Could your abilities as a differently thinking scientist provide a breakthrough that alleviates great suffering? Could your gifts in music draw other people to understand their spiritual side, or find a healthy outlet for their emotions? Could your business brain create jobs in companies that are run with great integrity? Could you write something that helps others to understand that there's a God who loves them?

I believe this is one of the key questions for all of us as we think about the journey of our lives: what gifts and passions has God given to me that I can give back to him?

I see my friends doing this all the time. I think of one who writes wonderful spoken-word poems, and performs them in schools and on video to help girls to navigate their teenage years. Or another who writes and directs films, and has used his gifts to bring people closer to God in cinemas all over the world. I have a friend who launched a charity that has an impact on kids and young people through sports coaching, where they teach positive values alongside the sport; now his organization connects with 12,000 people a week. I have another friend who has dedicated her life to working with the homeless and with drug addicts, and whose centre is literally saving lives every week.

These are just ordinary people, but they're working in partnership with an extraordinary God, and through them the world is being made just a little bit more like it was always meant to be. Through these people, God is making all things new, and he wants to do it through you and me too.

*

In every discipline imaginable, followers of Jesus have been involved in making the world better, working with God to move the world another step forward.

William Wilberforce, the great social justice campaigner, was motivated by his faith to work tirelessly for the abolition of slavery in most of the British Empire. He met regularly with a group of friends who called themselves 'the Clapham Sect', and these meetings – during which they prayed with and encouraged one another – provided the foundation for all of their social reform. By the time Wilberforce died, he'd advanced the cause not only of freedom but also of the alleviation of poverty, of animal welfare and more.

Florence Nightingale, regarded by many as the founder of modern nursing, spent years praying to God for a task that would define her life. Eventually she realized that the answer lay in her natural gift for caring for the sick, and, after going against her family's wishes, she became a nurse and ended up at the heart of organizing the medical service in the middle of a major war. By listening to God, exploring the gifts that he had given her and then following his lead, she made a huge impact on the medical profession that means her name remains famous 200 years after her birth.

Martin Luther King Jr, the American civil rights leader and Christian minister, was driven and sustained by his deep relationship with God. His famous speeches, which have now gone down in history as some of the greatest ever given, drew heavily on the Bible, and his deep ideology of non-violent protest was inspired by Jesus. It's impossible to separate Dr King's activism from his faith; each one drove the other forward.

Those three famous names don't even give you the half of it. There's **William and Catherine Booth**, founders of the Salvation Army – a movement that continues to help millions of the most vulnerable people around the world; **Mother Teresa**, who brought help and hope to some of the poorest people on earth; **Dag Hammarskjöld**, who as secretary-general of the United Nations in the 1950s, used his position to 'champion the underdog'. All of these people and millions of others throughout history have joined with God to accomplish something incredible in the creative re-making of the world. And if these people used their gifts to create structural change, many others have used their artistic abilities to begin to redecorate the world with a vibrant new layer of paint. Musicians from **Bach** through to **Elvis Presley**; actors like **Chris Pratt** and **Naomi Scott**. All of them embraced the divine creative spark and joined God on an adventure.

*

It seems fitting to end this book with a list of great Christian heroes, because if there's one thing we know about all of them it's that none of them are or were perfect. They share that in common with the amazing list of heroes found in the Bible in Hebrews 11, where the author reels off all the great characters found in the history of God's people. They were humans, just like us, all with plenty of flaws; all prone to messing up, getting it wrong and letting themselves and others down.

What they also all have in common, however, is that God stood at the very centre of their lives. He wasn't an optional extra, or even a strong preference. He was the sun, they were the moon. These people understood their lives, their relationship with God, as an orbit around him.

That is what I believe God wants to invite us to today. Not to be content with a faith where God is just another part of our lives, but to understand him as being part of *everything*. Like all the heroes who go before us, we are not perfect. But we *are* satellites, in orbit around God, who is at the very centre of our lives and of all things.

Don't crash into the sea in a ball of fire

When I first started toying with the idea of using a satellite as a metaphor for the Christian life, I did a bit of internet research on them. I saw a video of a NASA space rocket that was meant to be launching a US$280 million satellite into orbit. As you might imagine from my use of the words 'meant to', that's not exactly what happened. Something went wrong in the launch, where the various parts of the rocket failed to separate properly, and as a result the satellite ended up falling to earth again at the centre of a US$280 million fireball. Thankfully, it landed in the middle of the ocean, but I imagine it was never seen again.

This book might appear to contain a lot of 'shoulds'. You should pray; you should join a church and worship there; you should ask God for his Spirit; you should be reaching your friends, fighting injustice and learning worship guitar. If that's what you've read from these pages, then I'm sorry, because that was never my intention.

So let me, in my last few words, try again. God loves you. He wants to know you personally, and he wants to be at the centre of your life because, honestly, for your sake, that's the best place for him to be. That's it.

Now, there are lots of other things to explore in the Christian faith. None of them, though, are meant to be a burden; an extra layer of stuff to have to contend with. None of it is meant to layer you with guilt, or weigh you down with worry that you're a second-class Jesus follower. All of it is by invitation. By all means try to put the ideas in this book into practice, but take it gently. Be kind to yourself if you don't turn into the apostle Paul overnight.

Many Christians throughout history have ended up burnt out by religion, tired out by expectation or shamed because they didn't get it all right on the first try. That's not what Jesus wants. He said himself: 'my yoke is easy and my burden is light' (Matthew 11.30).

He doesn't want you to end up in a fireball over the ocean. He wants to send you into orbit, and then help you to stay there for the rest of your life. That's why he always makes the same simple offer, with no additional complication: 'Come, follow me.' The rest will come in time; for now, all he needs is for you to take his hand.

So, will you?